The New Encyclopedia for RVers

by Joe and Kay Peterson

RoVers Publications
Livingston, Texas

Products and services listed here are not endorsed by the authors, nor are they the only ones available in their particular categories.

Copyright© 1996
Encyclopedia for RVers
First printing, January 1988
Second printing September 1988
Third printing, February 1989

Revised editions
July 1989, January 1992, January 1996

ISBN 0-910449-07-4

Resource reference book. Contains addresses and phone numbers for RV-related products/services. Index included.

Direct questions regarding this book to:
Editorial Department
RoVers Publications
100 Rainbow Drive
Livingston, Texas 77351
(800) 976-8377
(409) 327-3019
Fax: 409-327-4388

Printed and bound in the United States of America.

CONTENTS

TIPS and HINTS

ADDRESSES AND TELEPHONE NUMBERS

MANUFACTURERS

PUBLICATIONS

ORGANIZATIONS

GOVERNMENT SERVICES

SERVICES FOR RVERS

SPECIAL INTEREST

8

Preface by Joe & Kay Peterson

The New Encyclopedia for RVers is divided into two sections. The first part deals with condensed reports on how to care for your equipment, ways to handle some of the lifestyle problems of extensive RV travel, and a potpourri of tips and hints, many of which were taken from *Escapees* magazine. If you find these tips to be as valuable as we do, you may want to find out more about the Escapees Club and its other benefits. You can do this by calling *1-800-9-ROVERS* and asking for the packet of free information.

The yellow pages, like the yellow pages of a phone book, contain names, addresses, and phone numbers of many types of products and services relating to the RV life. Here you will find both commonly needed and specialized sources that cover everything from A to Z—from AAA headquarters to Zip Dee awnings.

Every book that lists sources—as this one does— will have some material that was outdated the day that it is printed. Addresses change. Businesses are sold and, even though a change of address is filed with the U.S. Postal Service, those changes are only good for a few months.

If you send for a catalog or information and your letter comes back *Forwarding Expired,* please write to us . We may have a more current contact or may be able to find one. Even if we can't help you, we *want* to know of all errors so that we can correct them in future editions. We will also appreciate your sending us additional addresses that you feel would be of benefit to others when this book goes into its next printing.

The *Index* (white) section at the back of the book will help you to locate the addresses you need. If you don't know the name of the company you are trying to locate, look in the front *Contents* listing to determine the category which most closely matches the company for which you are searching.

We believe that *The New Encyclopedia For RVers* will become your most valuable RV reference book. Keep it handy so you can look up the services and products you need as you travel.

Part 1
Reports

Transmission/Engine Overheating

Bearings and seals are harmed by overheated fluid inside the transmission caused by towing heavy loads, wind resistance, and hill climbing. Transmission fluid travels to the radiator where the hot fluid passes through a small core within the radiator. Enough of the heat is transferred to the radiator fluid for average vehicle use, but not for pulling heavy loads. Each 20-degree increase above 175° F cuts the working life of transmission fluid in half. Excessive heat oxidizes the fluid and creates gum and varnish on the clutch plates and bands which leads to slippage. This in turn produces even more heat.

Signs of overheated transmission/engine

1. Transmission fluid line is too hot to touch.

2. Transmission dip stick smells like burnt toast.

3. You see oil spots on ground under your vehicle.

4. You feel your transmission "slipping."

5. You can hear the transmission thump into gear. People with shift kits *should* get a thump.

6. Oil pressure warning light comes on or the needle moves into the hot range.

7. Smoke can be seen coming from under the hood.

To correct overheating problem

1. If you don't have a transmission fluid cooler—buy the largest one available. This is a case of where bigger is better.

2. Flush and clean the cooling system every two years.

3. If there is any doubt that thermostat or radiator pressure caps are working properly, replace them.

If overheating continues after you have done the above, you may correct the problem by changing from the thermostatically controlled factory-built clutch fan to a larger mechanical fan. The thermostat-controlled clutch fan engages automatically when the temperature reaches a certain level. This uses less fuel and reduces noise, but when we are pulling heavier loads it doesn't always kick in soon enough. Better to get a little less gas mileage than harm the engine.

Automatic Transmission Maintenance

Manufacturers recommend changing transmission fluid after 100,000 miles. That's fine for vehicles being operated under normal conditions, but trailer towing, or driving a loaded motor home, is not under normal conditions. A transmission repair runs several hundred dollars but the cost of the preventative service is seldom more than $50. Therefore, preventative maintenance is the way to go.

Members of the Automatic Transmission Association (ATRA) recommend changing the filter (if it is the disposable type) *and* the transmission fluid every year or every 12,000 miles—whichever comes first.

Transmission authorities say automatic transmission fluid can wear out—just like a belt or a tire. Overheating can make the transmission fluid ineffective. Whenever you are pulling trailers or other heavy loads, or doing a lot of city driving, the fluid will overheat. Check your fluid at least every 1,000 miles.

Things to watch for

- If you are adding fluid frequently, your transmission may have a leak at a seal or gasket. Or it could be a malfunction in the transmission and its related components. Consult a certified transmission mechanic and then get a second opinion.

- If fluid has a burnt odor, or is dark brown, change the fluid.

- If you experience late or early shifting, slipping, or noises of any kind, immediately check with a transmission authority for economy and safety.

- Check your vehicle's cooling system regularly, and if you note excessive heat, have the situation remedied without delay.

- Know and abide by the manufacturer's recommendations for weight limits, loading, and trailer towing.

- When you suspect trouble, look for an ATRA transmission sign, which indicates a certified mechanic. A good transmission mechanic can diagnose problems without having to remove the transmission.

Jumper Cables

Batteries produce hydrogen gas as a by-product of the chemical reaction that takes place inside them. If you get the right combination of hydrogen and oxygen reacting with the spark when you jump start, an explosion may result which can cause serious acid burns or severe eye injury. If acid splatters into your eyes, immediately flush them with water for ten to fifteen minutes before you seek medical help.

How to jump-start a vehicle

1. Never smoke while jump-starting a vehicle!
2. Make sure the two vehicles do not touch each other.
3. Both electrical systems must be the same voltage.
4. Leave hood raised for a few minutes so gas can disperse before attempting to start the vehicle.
5. Clamp one end of one jumper cable to the *POSITIVE* terminal of the *dead* battery and the other end to the *POSITIVE* terminal of the *booster* battery. Don't allow the positive cable clamps to touch any metal other than the battery terminals.
6. Connect one end of the second cable to the *NEGATIVE* terminal of the *booster* battery and the other end to the engine block or frame of the stalled vehicle *not the negative post of the battery.* Be sure that this connection is away from the battery, carburetor, the fuel line, tubing, or any moving parts.
7. Stand out of the paths of both vehicles.
8. Start the vehicle with the *GOOD* battery first and then start the disabled vehicle.
9. Remove cables in *REVERSE ORDER*: start with the one clamped to the engine block or frame.
10. Another safe method is to connect the cables to the dead battery first, then with the engine running on the vehicle with the good battery, make the final connections. With the air movement generated from the radiator fan all accumulated hydrogen gases will have been dispersed.
11. Never attempt to jump-start a battery if the fluid in the battery is frozen.

Cylinder Compression Test

Although you seldom read about it, you should be doing periodic cylinder compression checks, especially when you are having any type of engine trouble. It is a simple test and will tell you the true shape of your engine. All it takes is a little of your time and a compression gauge that costs about $10.

How to do the test

Remove plugs, one cylinder at a time, and press the compression gauge into the spark plug hole. If you get a low reading on one or more of them, it means you either have bad rings or bad valves—or both.

If a cylinder shows weak on the compression gauge, give it several squirts of oil, and then take the pressure again. If the compression registers all right now, it means the problem is with the rings. But if the compression still registers low, it means the problem is with the valves.

Some people like to keep a record of each pressure check both wet and dry (with and without oil). If you want to do this, include the odometer reading.

If you are having engine trouble, take your own compression check as it will save money on unnecessary tune-ups. There are mechanics who will sell you a tune-up even when they know the basic problem is bad compression. And some mechanics are just too lazy to bother doing a compression check—especially if they know you are a traveler with whom they will probably never have to do business again.

Buying a used vehicle?

If you are purchasing a used vehicle, always get a compression test on it. Just listening to an engine is not enough. An engine that has almost zero compression on one cylinder can still sound all right even though it needs a major repair shortly.

Most people who work on their own engines will have no trouble pulling plugs. Normally, it is less than a 30 minute job although some engines take longer than others.

Engine Tips From *Escapees* magazine
From Mike Ashcraft, mechanic, writer and lecturer

- Chevrolet dealers carry the parts you need to combat faulty starter operation due to a hot engine compartment and high ambient temperatures. First, get a heavy-duty starter spring. Then add a starter solenoid heat shield and a starter motor support brace. If that doesn't do it, you'll have to go with the ultimate solution—GM's remote magnetic switch.

- To store your oil filler spout, try an old tennis-ball container with a plastic cap. The can will keep the spout from dripping residue all over, and the cap will keep dirt from accumulating on the spout between oil fills.

- Guaranteed vacuum connections: Use short lengths of shrink tubing over the connection. The connection will remain flexible and shrink tubing will ensure a good seal, especially in cases where the vacuum hose is a little loose on the fitting.

- With both metric and standard hardware on trucks these days, you may need an odd-size wrench. Nickels, dimes, or quarters often fit exactly into the space between the open end wrench and the smaller nut.

- The degreasers available in any auto parts store will remove light grease, but won't get all the grease off a really dirty spot such as the undercarriage. A household oven cleaner will strip off even heavy, caked-on grease down to the metal. Just follow the instructions on the can.

- Draining your radiator is always a pain in the neck because it never runs into the drain pan without first splashing on the suspension. A simple solution is to install a 90-degree spark plug boot over the end of the petcock. The fluid will be directed into your pan. If you can't find one that fits snugly, a small clamp will hold it in place.

- After you top off your transmission fluid from a full quart can, carrying it around is a nuisance. If you put the leftover fluid in an empty, *clean,* one-half quart dish-washing soap bottle, you will have a handy container with a spout you can close. But don't forget to label the bottle!

Engine Tips From *Escapees* magazine
From Mike Ashcraft, mechanic, writer and lecturer

• A variety of methods have been developed for holding the GMC 454 fuel pump rod out of the way while installing a new fuel pump. The most expedient method is to simply coat the fuel pump rod with a liberal amount of heavy axle grease. Slip it in and the grease will hold it in place while you install the pump.

• If you suspect a cracked distributor cap but don't want to replace it unless you're certain it is bad, look for small cracks in the cap or rotor by spraying some lighter fluid on the inside of the cap. The chemical makeup of lighter fluid will find its way through the smallest cracks and show up as a damp spot.

• If battery leaks occur around the terminal post, coat the plate on the terminal post with a silicone rubber product. This will keep a boiling battery from blowing fluid out around the terminal post.

• Using Teflon tape as a thread sealant is a thing of the past now that sealant manufacturers have come up with a liquid Teflon sealant for threaded connections. Used sparingly, it will eliminate the problem of debris (caused when using Teflon tape) from entering your fuel or oiling systems. A little dab'll do ya!

• Do your fan belts squeak? A few well-placed dabs of your favorite toothpaste on the contact faces of the belts will reduce the noise. The slight abrasive action of the toothpaste will eliminate the glaze that occurs after extended use.

• To find out if there has been a recall on your vehicle, write to:

National Highway Traffic Safety Administration
Department of Transportation
Washington, DC 20590
or call their hot line:
1-800-424-9393

RV Refrigerator and How It Works

The absorption refrigerator is an intricate system that we take for granted—until it quits working. When that happens, the chances are that we have either neglected or abused it because we don't really understand how the absorption system works. Unlike the compressor type we have lived with all these years, an absorption reefer uses heat to circulate a refrigerant.

Ammonia is the refrigerant used because its ability to absorb heat is most effective in the limited space of a sealed absorption system.

A boiler (or generator) sits at the bottom and holds a mixture of ammonia, water, and sodium chromate. When heat is applied to the boiler, either by propane or an electrical element, the ammonia turns into a vapor and rises through a percolator tube until it eventually passes into the water separator tube.

Cool water, circulating around the water separator tube, causes any water in the ammonia to condense. The water returns to the boiler; the ammonia vapor continues on to the condenser. The fins on the condenser accelerate cooling and cause the ammonia vapor to liquefy again.

The liquid ammonia passes into an evaporator (the part that extends into the freezer compartment) where it meets hydrogen, again causing it to evaporate. As this evaporation takes place, the heat inside the refrigerator is absorbed through the walls of the looped pipe.

Now both the hydrogen and ammonia gases pass into the absorber where the ammonia returns once again to liquid. As it liquefies, it releases heat that is carried off by the circulating air. The hydrogen, now free of the weight of the ammonia, rises and returns to the evaporator.

The liquid ammonia passes down into the absorption chamber where it is collected. When the chamber fills, the ammonia flows into the exit tube and returns to the boiler for recycling.

Because of the intricate system, it is essential that the evaporator coil remains level to prevent the liquid from forming pockets when more cooling is needed.

Taking Proper Care of Refrigerator

1. Always level refrigerator. When traveling, the continuous movement keeps the absorption type refrigerator working; but if you park so that the evaporator coil in the refrigerator is not level, the liquid will form pockets which block the gas circulation. This not only causes the cooling to stop, but over a period of time, there is an accumulative effect that will eventually cause the system to shut down permanently.

Don't use the floor or a counter top in the rig to test for level. Their being level isn't proof of a level refrigerator. The recommended method is to level with the bubble in the freezer.

Tip: To avoid having to open freezer door each time you level: first level with the bubble in freezer, then find a convenient place in your RV where the bubble is also level. Use that to level afterwards. Another way is to glue the bubble on the *outside* door of the refrigerator after you make sure the refrigerator is level. Then just check the bubble each time you level after that.

2. Door seal must fit snugly against the frame on all sides of the door or your refrigerator will not cool properly. Seals dry out. To check the seal, place a sheet of paper on refrigerator box so that when you shut the door the paper is trapped between the two surfaces. The door should grip the paper so firmly that it is difficult to slide it out. If it slides out easily—buy new gaskets from the manufacturer. They are not difficult to replace. Some types slip into a groove, some must be cemented in place, and some are held with screws.

6. Defrost as needed. The thermostat capillary tube (a silver wire with a rounded tip located under the freezer compartment) tells the refrigerator when to start and stop working. If this wire gets frosted over it will send a signal to shut off when actually more cooling is needed.

Helping Your Refrigerator

If you have trouble getting the refrigerator to cool properly, the tendency is to turn the knob to the maximum setting. But this aggravates the problem instead of correcting it. Turn the setting back to number five (medium) until the trouble is corrected.

Summer can be hard on absorption refrigerators. If the cooling problem occurs during extremely hot weather, it may be that there is not enough cool air circulating to push the heat up the vent chamber. Before you get involved in the troubleshooting procedures on the following page, try increasing the air movement.

Prop the access panel door wide open. Place a portable fan on a chair facing it so that the air blows directly across the back of the refrigerator. This will help push that hot air up the vent chamber.

We purchased a small 12-volt fan of the type used in our ceiling vents and permanently mounted it inside the refrigerator access door. By attaching a cooling thermostat to it, this fan operates automatically when excessive heat calls for more air circulation. The electrical draw on batteries is minimal and it has corrected our refrigerator cooling problems.

You can also help your refrigerator in the summer if you try always to park so your refrigerator side does not get direct sun—especially the hot afternoon sun. If this is not possible and you have an awning on the refrigerator side, it will give some protection from the sun.

Don't overload your refrigerator, especially in hot weather. The fewer items there are in the box, the better the cool air can circulate.

Items that need to be the coldest should be placed in the bottom section of the refrigerator. The upper door shelves are the warmest part of the refrigerator.

Always level your refrigerator, even on short stops.

Trouble-Shooting Refrigerator

- **Thermocouple out of adjustment:** If you have trouble lighting the pilot, readjust the thermocouple. It should be positioned directly over the flame.

- **Faulty thermostat:** This isn't a common problem, but if the refrigerator works fine on electric but not on gas, it means the gas thermostat needs replacing. Also, check the LP thermostat. As you turn gas knob from low to high, it is working all right if you see an increase in size of the flame.

- **Faulty electric element:** If the refrigerator works on gas but not on electric, the heater element is probably at fault. Check it with an ohmmeter. It should read between 65 and 100 ohms if it is working properly.

- **Check for heat to the boiler**. Open the outside panel so you can see the backside of the refrigerator. Feel the boiler to see if it is hot. If it isn't, it isn't working properly. If the coil isn't hot when operating on electricity, switch the circuit breakers on and off a few times and it may correct the problem. If not, get help.

- **Pilot blowout** is a common problem with older RVs due to down drafts. New units have blowout baffles. Correct the problem by installing a down draft kit (from manufacturer).

- **Check vent channel.** Dirt in the flue causes the refrigerator to stop cooling. While the access panel is open, take a four-inch mirror and position it so you can see clear up the back side to the roof vent (vent channel). If it is not clear and open, the hot air cannot escape out the top.

You can clean the flue assembly through the access door at the back of the refrigerator. Or remove the roof vent cover, reach down and extract the long baffle in the flue, then stick a brush attached to a long piece of something, such as a rifle cleaning rod or an old piece of TV antenna, and ream out the flue.

Tip: Soot will fall on burner causing a mess unless you cover it first. Also, put a suction hose end from a vacuum cleaner near the bottom end of the flu. Turn the vacuum on before you start reaming so that the vacuum will suck up the soot.

Air Conditioner Maintenance

To keep the seals from drying out, run the air conditioner every two weeks year-round for at least 15 minutes each time.

Clean the shroud and the filter monthly when the air conditioner is not in use, and weekly when it is being used. Dirty filters lessen the cooling effect and can cause the evaporator coils to freeze up. Also, bacteria builds up on the filter and every time you turn the air conditioner on, the bacteria are forced into the air. This is especially true in humid areas. The result can be severe respiratory problems, especially for people with allergies. The shroud and filter are accessible from inside the RV and are simple to remove. Clean them with hot soapy water, rinse well, and dry before replacing.

Check the evaporator coils annually to see if they need cleaning. To do this, you'll have to remove the air conditioner cowling which may be either inside or outside. Clean with a stiff bristle brush and hot soapy water.

This is a good time to check the roof gasket around the air conditioner to see if it needs replacing. All gaskets will harden and compress with time. When this happens to the air conditioner gasket, it may cause a rain leak which you may not realize is from this source. If you have a leak, this is one place to check. If the gasket shows signs of cracking or looks suspicious, it is best to change it even if you don't yet have a leak.

Procedure for replacing the Seal

1. Shut off all electrical power to the air conditioner.
2. Four bolts secure the air conditioner to the roof and compress the gasket. Remove these bolts and you can tilt the air conditioner to one side.
3. If you have a heat strip, you'll need to remove the sheet metal cover at the bottom (six sheet metal screws hold it in place) and disconnect the cable to the heat unit.
4. For best results, use a replacement gasket of the same type that the manufacturer used. Check with a local RV store for replacement. It may have to be ordered for you.

RV Roof Maintenance

Resealing your RV roof should be an annual maintenance chore instead of waiting for a leak to develop. It is not a difficult procedure, although it does take a bit of time and the proper materials.

1. It is essential to thoroughly clean the roof of any old sealer before resealing. The easiest way is to start at a spot where the edges have begun to lift or are beginning to crack. Scrape off the old sealer with a putty knife, being careful not to gouge or cut into the exterior skin when scraping. Use a wire brush on stubborn parts and to "roughen" all areas where you will put the new sealer to help it stick better and make it last longer.

2. When all surfaces are clean and dry, apply the sealer with a brush or caulking gun following manufacturer's instructions.

3. After applying the sealer, do not wash the coach for several days in order to allow the sealant to cure.

Helpful Hints

- Determine the type of sealer that the manufacturer originally used and use the same type. Generally, it is either a fibrous coating or a rubbery compound. The fibrous type is like a thick paint and is usually applied with a brush while the rub-bery compound is applied with a caulking gun. If you are not sure of the type, check with your dealer.

- If the roof vents are cracked or brittle, replace them *before* you start resealing.

- While you are working on the seams, inspect all the areas of the roof for pin holes or punctures.

- Be careful not to apply too much sealer around the TV antenna as it can prevent the antenna from rotating properly.

- If the air conditioner needs to be resealed, be sure to replace the rubber gasket. (Purchase at any RV store.)

WARNING! If your RV has a soft roof as opposed to the laminated type, you should use a board both to walk and kneel on so you won't step on an unsupported area.

RV Awning

RV manufacturers usually list an awning as optional equipment, but most of us consider them to be necessary. There are two types. The less common is the pole and stake awning, which costs about half the price of the roll-ups. It is generally used only by RVers who leave their rig set up in one place for prolonged periods because it requires a network of poles, stakes, and braces (called guys) to support the fabric canopy. When moving, this type must be disassembled and transported inside the RV until you get to the next campground. It takes about twenty minutes and usually requires two people to set it up.

Most RVers prefer a roll-up type because one person can put it up or take it down in about two minutes. It rolls up like a window shade around a spring-loaded tube which is securely attached to the side of the RV and then locked into place for travel. The fabric on roll-up awnings is made of durable easy-care synthetic acrylic fibers or a vinyl or woven acrylic.

Cleaning

Manufacturers recommend that you regularly clean the fabric with a detergent and warm water. This is especially important if you are parked under trees where sap, pine needles, or bird droppings falling on the awning cause stains. Regular washing is essential in areas where *mildew* is a problem.

To combat mildew, add one cup of bleach to every two gallons of warm water. Scrub the affected areas with a soft brush and then rinse well. Don't roll the awning back into casing until it is thoroughly dry. Make sure to rinse off the side of your RV if any bleach has splashed or run down. Vinyl is not affected by mildew if it is kept clean, so if you wash your awning fabric every month, you should have no mildew problem.

Awning Magic (by Carefree of Colorado) and *Mighty Bright Awning Cleaner* (Faulkner Manufacturing Co.) are available in most RV supply stores. They do not work any better than bleach, but some people find them easier to use.

Care of RV Awning

- **Wind damage:** A severe wind storm can rip the fabric or cause the fabric to rip loose from the hardware. It can also bend the arms. When you are parked in areas where sudden wind or rain storms are likely to occur, *never* leave your awning out when you are away from the rig. Since it only takes a minute or two to roll it up, it is better to be safe.

- **Rain damage:** Rain causes just as much damage as wind. Pitch the awning with one side lowered to allow rain runoff. Even when this is done, during an excessively heavy rain, the water may collect faster than it can run off. Once this happens, your fabric develops a sag that gets worse with each succeeding rain.

- **Bent hardware:** The weight of the pooled rain can also bend the supports. Bent roller tubes, rafter bars, or shaft cannot be repaired; they must be replaced. That is an expensive penalty for forgetting to roll up an awning.

- **Dry awning before rolling it up:** A rolled up wet awning encourages mildew growth. If you roll it up during heavy rain, put it out again as soon as possible and thoroughly hose it down.

- **Correct sag:** Sag develops with age especially on awnings over 15 feet—even if you are careful not to allow the fabric to collect rain pockets. Sag can usually be corrected by adding a center rafter support which can be ordered at an RV supply store or from the manufacturer.

- **Lubricate as necessary:** Lightly lubricate the pins, bearing locks, push buttons, and pull rings. Better not to use WD-40 as it tends to stain the fabric. Zip Dee recommends using a clear silicone lubricant instead; A&E Systems suggest using paraffin wax on the support arms and rafter arms for a smooth sliding movement.

- **Before traveling:** Make sure the locks and pins are in place. If an awning is not secured, it can shake loose during travel, damaging the awning and possibly causing an accident.

Caution: Don't grill or barbecue underneath your awning—the animal fat causes stains that cannot be removed.

Replacing Your RV Carpet

You can give your RV a face-lift with new carpet. First, decide how much you need. Measure the space carefully. When you are figuring the number of square yards, don't forget to include closets and other special areas. Get a little more than you think you need.

When you start shopping, look for a quality that will stand up to the high density traffic pattern of your RV, but don't look for a carpet that will "last forever." You'll change it in a few years when you need another face-lift.

The cost of replacing carpet is minimal because you don't need much and because you can look for roll ends. These rolls, left over after a big job, normally sell for about half the price of carpet on a full roll. Don't hesitate to negotiate instead of accepting the quoted price as final. You might get it for less.

Select a different color than you had before. Light, solid colors look lovely when new, but they show every bit of dirt. Your carpet will look good longer if you select one that has several shades of color or even several colors.

You may find the quote for installation very high because many installers have not done RV carpets. They are used to doing big square floors that require very little cutting and fitting. Some may try to convince you that you can do it yourself. You can. It takes time, but you do have plenty of that, don't you?

Procedure for installing carpet

Lay the new carpet face down on a patio or similar smooth, clean surface. Remove the old carpet and lay it face down on top of the new carpet. Trace the pattern with a felt tip pen. Then cut the carpet with a single face razor blade. (You need it sharp so have plenty on hand.) Allow a two-inch border to be trimmed later. Where seams are necessary, put them together with glue using backing or a heavy material as the connecting section, or sew the seams with an upholstery needle.

You can rent a "carpet kicker" for a tighter fit.

Maintenance of Waste Disposal System

- Sewer hoses tend to develop pin holes. A bit of vinyl tape and a drop of vinyl cement do a good patch job.

- If you can't get the elbow on a new sewer hose, pour hot water over the end of the hose, or soak it in a bucket of hot water, and it will slip right on.

- Never push the sewer hose more than a few inches into a park sewer outlet. If it goes in too deep, it can prevent the sewage flow through the main line.

- Purchase a coupling and a 20-foot sewer hose. Cut hose into two *unequal* lengths. Use the shortest one that will reach. The coupling will allow you to put the two sections together in case you need the full 20 feet.

- When using hookups, leave the black water (sewer) dump valve closed. Dump only when the holding tank gets full or when you are ready to travel. If you leave the valve open, the liquids will flow out leaving built-up solids behind. When you dump when the tank is full, the volume of liquids will carry solids with them. It is okay to leave the gray water (sink water) valve open.

- Dump the holding tank before taking a shower or bath so bath water can rinse out the sewer hose.

- When dumping, be careful not to close the valve until all the waste runs out. If the handle is pushed in while the waste is emptying, paper and solids can be forced into the track which will cause leakage. Make sure you close the valve all the way.

- After dumping, flush the tank well. You can purchase a wand to attach to the shower or water hose for this. Simply push the wand through the toilet into the tank, turn on the water, and rotate the wand so water pressure cleans out the corners.

- Keep the rods on black and gray water flappers at the holding tank outlets well lubricated with a graphite lubricant.

- To minimize buildup of grease in the drain pipe, dispose of all grease by pouring it in throwaway containers with lids. Just before traveling, pour white distilled vinegar down the sink drain. Sloshing motion helps cut grease buildup in the waste water tank.

Macerator Pump

A macerator is a small pump, powered by a 12-volt electric motor, that can liquefy your sewage from the black water tank and pump that liquid through a garden hose into a toilet or clean-out drain even if the drain is several feet higher than the RV sewage outlet.

The pump is three inches round by eight inches long (including the pump and motor), so it takes up very little room. Camping World was selling them for around $100. Any marine or RV store can order one for you from the manufacturer. (See addresses.)

You can also use a macerator when you have hookups to speed up the emptying process. In either case, the black water (sewage tank) should always be pumped first so that your gray water (sink water) will clean out the pump and hose.

The directions that come with the macerator say that you must not use a hose smaller in diameter than one inch. One-inch hoses are very difficult to find and are very expensive. We have been using a 5/8-inch hose for ten years with no problem, and we know of other boondockers who do the same.

Nevertheless, we *recommend* using a Gates 3/4-inch rubber hose because it has a larger diameter, it is stiffer, it does not collapse as easily, and it is less likely to get mixed up with your fresh water hoses. The problem is that this size is also hard to find.

When you are ready to mount your macerator, you need to attach it directly to the RV sewer outlet. Your RV came from the factory with a blank plastic cover that prevents sewage from dripping out in the event your discharge valves are not completely closed. This plastic cover can be attached permanently to your macerator so that the unit can be taken on and off as easily as the blank cover.

See the following page for mounting directions.

How to Mount a Macerator

1. Drill a 1 1/4-inch hole in the center of the plastic cover that came with your RV.

2. Remove the four bell nuts from the outlet end of the macerator.

3. Put the plastic cover against the outlet side of the macerator and align the hole you drilled in it with the 1 1/4-inch hole in the macerator.

4. Very carefully mark the cover at the four points where the studs contact it. (The studs are what the bell nuts were screwed into.)

5. Drill the cover at the four marked locations. Use a drill bit slightly larger than the studs.

6. Before securing the cover to the macerator, spread a layer of silicone between the two. Tighten the bell nuts and allow the silicone to dry thoroughly before you trim the excess from around the 1 1/4-inch-hole.

After you have mounted the macerator pump, the last step is to wire it to your 12-volt power using Number 14 (or larger) wire. Some folks clip it onto their battery terminals with alligator clamps and run an extension cord, but here's a better way:

Install a 12-volt outlet near the sewer outlet so you can simply plug your macerator in when you need it. Make sure that you are tapping into a 20-amp or larger circuit as the pump draws 16 amps when it is under a load.

You need a quick way to disconnect the macerator. You can buy a 12-volt disconnect plug for about a dollar at an auto parts or Radio Shack store. Wire the plug into the line at the pump so that it can be used to turn the motor off and on, thereby eliminating the need for a switch.

LP Gas Regulator

Moisture can get into the LP gas regulator. When it does and the temperature goes below freezing, any moisture (water) in the regulator will freeze. The result is that it can stop the flow of gas on a freezing day when you need it most, or it can cause the regulator to malfunction.

When a regulator doesn't function properly, it sometimes allows tank pressure to enter the lines, and this in turn can cause a fire or an explosion.

Sometimes frozen water in the regulator will crack the regulator case, and you don't even know about it until it warms up and the smell of escaping gas catches your attention.

Propane can stand a tremendously lower temperature than butane. The problem for RVers is that they may buy butane in a southern state and then travel to a northern state where the butane would freeze. But usually if your LP gas stops flowing in the winter— during or after freezing weather— the regulator has frozen. In most cases it will thaw out without causing problems.

Ways to help your regulator

1. If the regulator is mounted with the vent facing up or toward the side, moisture is more apt to seep into the ambient side of the diaphragm inside the regulator. Make sure your regulator is positioned so that the vent is turned down, so that any moisture will have a chance to drain out.

2. If your regulator is not in an enclosed compartment, install an LP regulator protective cover to prevent rain and splashes from getting into your regulator.

3. If you store your rig in a place where the temperature may drop below freezing, it is best to turn off the main supply valve at the tank. Then if the regulator does freeze and crack, you won't have gas escaping when it thaws out.

4. Watch for signs of a malfunctioning regulator. These are most visible at the cook stove. Be on the lookout for an abnormally high or low flame, a sputtering flame, or a flame that doesn't remain steady.

Testing For LP Gas Leaks

Most of us have a valve that automatically switches from one LP tank to the other when a tank empties. This gives us a simple method for checking for LP gas leaks which should be a regular part of our maintenance program.

Test Procedure: Shut off all LP appliances and pilots. Now there is no gas flow, but the indicator on your tank will still show pressure in the lines. Next, shut off the gas valves at the tanks. If there are no leaks, the indicator will continue to show pressure in the lines for several hours. Check the indicator every half hour for two hours. If the indicator shows that a tank is empty, you have a leak in the system. In this case, turn the gas back on from the tank you were using and test every fitting with dish-washing detergent until you find the place where bubbles appear (usually at the joints around the fittings). Retighten the fitting. Be careful not to twist anything else as you tighten the flare nut.

If tightening the nut doesn't correct it, there is something wrong in the line itself or you have a cracked flare nut. If you don't know how to correct it, go to a repair facility before you use your LP gas system.

When you think you have corrected the problem, repeat the test. This time you must turn on the gas from the tank you've been using, and then turn it off again. If there are no other leaks, the indicator should show a continuing gas pressure within the lines.

Never smoke or use matches while testing for leaks!

CAUTION: There is a danger in filling gasoline tanks when your pilot lights are on. As the liquid gasoline goes in, it pushes air and fumes out of the tank. Usually these fumes are diluted enough by the surrounding air to render them harmless within a few feet, but wind, or the lack of it, can make the gasoline fumes wander further. If they contact a pilot light, an explosion could result.

When the experts say "turn off the LP gas," they do not mean the main tank valves. LP gas stays in the lines for a few minutes keeping the pilots burning, so you need to *turn off all the pilot lights!*

Cleaning Fresh Water System

Mineral deposits form inside RV pipes and tanks even if you use filters. You need to flush the system at least once a year with a mixture of water and either household bleach or white vinegar.

First, you'll need to fill several containers with clean water as you will be without water for several hours. Then turn off the outside water supply and drain your fresh water tank and your water heater. Open all the water faucets—hot and cold. Run the pump until all the lines are empty and faucets start sputtering air.

Immediately turn off the pump. Close all faucets and the drain valve on both the fresh water tank and the water heater. If you use vinegar, dilute by half. If you use bleach (preferred for the first time that you clean your water system) dilute by one gallon of bleach to ten gallons of water. You will need enough solution to fill up your water lines and your water heater.

Now, turn on the pump. It should come on briefly and then stop. Continue adding solution until the pump pushes water instead of air. Then open *one* faucet until you can smell or taste the solution mixture. Shut the faucet and proceed in the same manner with all the remaining faucets. Then shut off the pump.

Wait two to four hours so the mixture has time to dissolve the impurities in the pipes, lines, and tanks. Don't skimp on solution or time if you want a good job.

Now empty the fresh water tank and then fill it with plain water. Dump it again. Fill tank a second time, but only half full. Turn on the pump. Then start opening one faucet at a time (pump should come on) until the water runs clear and tastes good. (When the water is palatable, you've rinsed enough that any bleach in water won't harm you.) When you've done this at all the faucets, drain the rest of the water out of the fresh water tank.

Fill fresh water tank for use, shut off the pump, and then turn on the outside water supply.

Neither vinegar nor bleach will harm RV pipes, valves, or gaskets. In future cleaning, you can use more water and less bleach.

The RV Battery

RV or deep-cycle batteries are made of the same materials as automotive batteries. The difference is that they have more active lead which is a critical storage substance. Batteries fail for several reasons:

1. Shorted or open cells: This results from excess vibration or warped plates caused by overcharging.

2. Sulfation: When a battery does not receive *full* recharge often enough, it will grow sulfate crystals within the plates. After a period of time, these sulfate crystals become irreversible so that a portion of the battery is forever lost to future storage capacity.

3. Contamination: Caused by adding impure water.

4. Shedding of the active lead material: The part of the battery that stores electricity is the active lead paste that is pressed into the gridwork of each plate. If this active lead shakes off and falls to the bottom of the case, it can block the circulation of the acid electrolyte.

A worn-out battery will always let you down when you put it under a load. Throw it away or trade it in.

How to get maximum battery life

1. Check level of electrolyte twice a month on new batteries and weekly on older ones. Add distilled water to the designated level, but avoid overfilling.

2. Keep the terminal connections and cables free from corrosion. At the first sign of corrosion, clean the battery terminals with a wire brush, being careful to protect your eyes and clothes. Make the terminals shine and then coat with Vaseline.

3. The proper way to check your battery's state of charge is with a hydrometer. A fully-charged battery will give a hydro-meter reading of 1.25 to 1.28 per cell.

4. If you aren't going to be using the battery for several weeks, fully charge it and then store in a cool, dry place. If you aren't going to use it for several months, you need to check or recharge it every two to three months during the period it isn't used.

Keep RV batteries indoors or protected. And remember, they need to be vented. Only the new sealed type do not need venting.

Solar Panels

Most people like the idea of being electrically independent, so when they see fellow RVers getting their electricity from the sun, their tendency is to purchase solar (photovoltaic) panels. The question you must ask yourself is, will you use them enough to make them worth the initial investment?

The answer to that depends on what type of an RVer you are. Solar panels pay for themselves very quickly if you use them to take advantage of free parking in coyote camps. They are convenient, but not necessary, for overnight parking without hookups. They are not worth the investment if you always stay in full-hookup parks and campgrounds. One possible exception is if you are staying for long periods in parks where you pay your own metered electricity.

A simple solar system consists of two solar panels, one extra battery, and a regulator to prevent overcharge and to control the amount of energy going into the battery. The cost for two 40-watt panels and accessories will be less than a thousand dollars. With a solar system of this size, you should be able to get by indefinitely without commercial hookups if you park in the sun. (Solar panels only get a trickle charge on cloudy and rainy days.)

A system of this size will allow full usage of your 12-volt lights, water pump, television, vacuum cleaner, sewing machine, and a computer. It will run a microwave oven or coffee pot for a short period. It will *not* run an electric heater or an air conditioner. If you spend a great deal of time boondocking and you want to use more electrical appliances, or several at one time, you may need another panel, another battery, and an adequate size inverter.

We recommend you start with just one solar panel (no extra battery or regulator needed for one panel) and then add the other components later if you find you need them. (See addresses for information and books on solar.)

The solar system has the advantage of not requiring maintenance beyond a few simple chores, such as brushing off accumulated leaves or washing dirt from the face of the solar panels. Having no electronic parts, they are virtually trouble-free. They require no fuel since the sun is the source of power to recharge your batteries. They make no noise.

Inverters

Inverters are often confused with **CON**verters. A **CON**verter is what came with your RV and it changes the 120-volt AC power to 12-volt DC power to charge your RV batteries and to operate your 12-volt lights, water pump, furnace etc. An **IN**verter does the opposite. It changes the 12-volt battery power to 120-volt AC so you can run a sewing machine, vacuum cleaner, TV, etc.

The primary benefit of an inverter-powered AC system is the convenience of instant, reliable power, without the noise, fumes, and vibration of a gasoline generator.

Types of inverters

Square Wave: This type is the most commonly used inverter. Most of them are manufactured by Tripp. They come in a wide variety of sizes from 50 to 1000 watts.

The only advantage to these inverters is that they are much cheaper than better designed, more complex inverters. The big disadvantage is that they are "square wave" which means a poor quality power that works adequately on a light bulb but is not efficient on an induction-type motor or on a 120-volt TV set. Another complaint is that they must be "sized" to the load. That means the inverter must be large enough for the load it is to be used with, but not too much bigger because the extra power is lost just as though it were actually being used.

Rotary inverter: This is a 12-volt motor that powers a 120-volt generator (actually an alternator). These are made by Honeywell and come in 500-watt and 1600-watt sizes. They produce a full sine wave and will run any type load. It is ideal for operating portable tools, such as electric saw, drill motor etc. Because of the full sine wave, it gives these tools the full power that they would have from standard 120-volt power.

An excellent feature with the Honeywell is that there is a demand start which means no battery drain when the electric tool is turned off. In other words, the Honeywell doesn't have to be turned on and off. The disadvantage is that it is very inefficient and will run down the RV batteries if you use it for long periods.

Modified sine wave: These newer, hi-tech, solid state inverters are large enough to run appliances such as a microwave for short periods. They will run every appliance in your RV except an air conditioner or electric heater.

They do not have the featured demand start of the rotary type, but they don't need it because, without a load, they pull only seven-hundredths of an amp. With such a low draw, they can stay on the line until needed without a noticeable demand on your batteries. They are called "modified sine wave" because an inverter cannot produce a full sine wave. That comes only from a generated power source, not an inverted one.

For every amp you use at 120 volts, you take more than 10 amps out of the battery. (One amp at 120 volts equals exactly the same power as ten amps at 12 volts—not counting the loss in converting 12 volts to 120 volts.) There is no such thing as an unlimited power source while self-contained; but when an inverter is used in conjunction with a battery-charging method such as driving or a light plant (generator), or better yet photovoltaic (solar) panels, your inverter can provide you with full-time power without the necessity of having a full time power supply.

Inverters and personal computers

Another advantage of these modified sine wave inverters is that they allow one to run a computer whether boondocking or using standard 120-volt hookups. With more RVers using personal computers, it is important to remember that public power is prone to surges, spikes, and loss of power due to storms. When the computer is running off an inverter, there is an uninterrupted power supply which completely isolates the computer from power disturbances.

Only the newer, hi-tech, solid-state modified-sine-wave-type inverters, such as the Heart Interface and Trace, can be safely used with computers because they are voltage and frequency regulated.

RV Lighting

The RV electrical system is powered by a converter which charges the batteries for the 12-volt system when you are not hooked up to "city" power. The 12-volt (DC) incandescent lamps (bulbs) are better made and they last longer than regular AC household bulbs. They also cost more.

The standard RV single-contact bayonet (#1141) lamp is the best. Experts recommend that you stay with these lamps and not buy the #1156 bulb sold everywhere because it is designed for a taillight. The #1156 may initially cost less, but is intended to be used while the engine is running. It draws over half an amp more than the #1141. This is definitely a consideration when you are operating on battery power. The dimes you save on the lower price of a #1156 are lost because you have to replace them far more often, as well as use up unnecessary battery power.

The 12-volt fluorescent fixture is the best bargain for RVs because it provides more light and over a wider area than an incandescent lamp. And it uses less amp draw.

Unfortunately, RV fluorescent fixtures have poor voltage regulation, so a power surge or high voltage can destroy the fluorescent ballast. It costs as much to replace the ballast as it does to buy a new fixture.

An RV is subject to power surges and periods of high voltage whenever it is hooked up to city power because both the 110-volt power line and the RV converter lack good voltage regulation capabilities. Power line problems pass on through the system. Also, whenever you turn a fluorescent light on there is a sudden rush of energy to the ballast.

Another disadvantage of fluorescent lights is that they produce radio waves which cause frequency interference with AM radio and short wave reception.

Fluorescent fixtures and lamps are available everywhere. The #1141 incandescent lamp can be purchased at RV stores and, since it is used in high-intensity fixtures, it can often be found in office supply stores.

Quartz-halogen lamps are incandescent lamps, but they have a "hotter" filament which means they will produce a brighter light.

They are actually filled with halogen gas that is enclosed in a quartz shell. The earlier quartz-halogen lamps that were available to RVers were extremely expensive and so sensitive to handling (body oil) that they either would not work at all or quickly burnt out. Another problem was that they did not fit our RV sockets, so we had to crimp the sockets in order to get them to work. These lamps were extremely hot when in use and even caused some plastic RV fixtures to melt. They had to be handled very carefully and used in a shielded fixture. Some of us were willing to put up with the many inconveniences because the quartz-halogen lamps put out so much light with no more amperage draw than ordinary incandescent lamps.

Now there is a new quartz-halogen lamp available that has low wattage and does not require the special handling and shielding that the original ones did. The new ones use very little electricity and should have a long life span. One 5-watt (1/2 amp) lamp provides enough light for normal activities. There are also new, improved adapters to make the lamps fit your RV fixtures.

Even the new quartz-halogen lamps are sensitive to power surges and high voltages such as when batteries are being charged. In the future, this should be corrected and experts predict a 20-watt size quartz-halogen lamp may well become the RV standard.

At this time, quartz-halogen lamps cost about $8 per lamp, but they last more than 5 times as long as a regular incandescent lamp, which may mean they will be cheaper in the long haul.

The new quartz-halogen lamps are sold in specialty lighting stores or you can order them by mail.

We recommend you send for mail order catalogs. See addresses in back of the book.

Hints On Electrical Troubleshooting

Know where your circuit breaker and fuse panels are located so you don't have to go searching for them in the dark. Label all circuits so you know which circuit goes to each appliance and fixture.

Keep spare fuses on hand. The little 12-volt fuses sometimes blow at one of the ends where you can't see it. If you can't get a 12-volt appliance or fixture to work, and you don't have a tester, go ahead and replace the fuse even though it appears to be good.

An inoperable 110-volt appliance may start working again if you switch circuit breakers off and on again several times.

Sometimes 12-volt light bulbs don't work properly because of rust and corrosion caused by dampness or condensation. Clean the lamp connections with sandpaper including the little lead tips at the contact tip of the light bulbs. Then coat lightly with Vaseline to prevent future oxidation.

Automotive-type circuit breakers are often used as safety devices in RVs. They will probably be fastened down with two screws and will have a metal strap spot-welded to the back.

Unlike the familiar 110-volt circuit breaker, which remains open after tripping until it is reset, the 12-volt automotive circuit breaker automatically resets a few seconds after it opens. It will continue to cycle open and closed until the overload current is reduced or until the breaker mechanism fails.

It is important that the circuit breaker be hooked up correctly. The source or "hot" wire should always be hooked to the terminal marked "batt" (battery). This is because the opposite terminal (sometimes marked "Aux") comes in contact with the metal case when the breaker opens. Whenever both wires are charged (hot), such as between a charging source (alternator) and a battery, or between two batteries, the circuit breaker must be insulated from the frame of the vehicle. This can be easily done by mounting the circuit breaker to a small piece of wood and then securing the wood to the vehicle.

Catalytic Heaters

The manufacturer of your RV calls his product "self-contained," but you'll find out it isn't— if you spend one cold night in it without hookups. You'll run your battery down using the factory-provided forced air furnace. RVers who depend on self-containment solve the problem by installing a catalytic heater which works in conjunction with the forced air furnace. You can run either or both, of them at the same time.

To appreciate this, you need to understand how a catalytic heater works. When LP gas and air are exposed to each other in the presence of a catalytic agent, it causes them to combine chemically. This chemical combination results in the release of heat. Unlike open-flame camping heaters, catalytic heaters don't produce harmful quantities of carbon monoxide (although they do consume oxygen) and they are completely silent.

Heat efficiency:

With a catalytic heater, all of the energy from the propane fuel is transformed into heat. With your conventional heater, about 50% of the heat is lost to the outside through the exhaust vent. If you doubt it, stand outside in front of the vent when the furnace is operating!

Cuts battery drain:

A conventional forced air furnace relies on an electric-powered fan to distribute the warm air. A catalytic heater produces a radiant type heat which does not require a fan to disperse the heat. The catalytic heater has *no* battery drain and does not even hook up to the 12-volt system.

The only disadvantage to a catalytic heater is that it adds moisture to the air which then condenses on the windows and walls. (See report on solving the condensation problem on the following page.)

Since Term-X is no longer on the market, we recommend the Olympian. It comes with the option of an oxygen-depletion sensor (O.D.S.). Since the sensor is subject to malfunction at high altitudes, we don't recommend the sensor. We haven't found a sensor to be necessary, so why spend the extra.

Dealing With Condensation

Condensation is a common RV problem during the winter because an RV has a smaller volume of air and more windows (percentage wise) than houses do. The tighter the construction (fewer cracks around windows and doors), the more controlled the ventilation.

Moisture on windows is a nuisance when it clouds visibility, but the real problem is that when you see it on the windows, you know it is also collecting on adjacent walls and floor surfaces. This can lead to mildew, staining and, in severe cases, rot.

When air at a given temperature cannot hold any more water vapor, we say it has a relative humidity of 100%. Lowering the temperature will force some of the vapor to condense as water. Condensation, then, is the result of an excessive moisture content of the air inside the RV. If you switch from a standard furnace to a catalytic heater, the condensation problem increases.

Ways to cut down on condensation

1. Reduce the source. Cooking is one of the prime culprits that adds moisture. If you keep cooking pots covered, less steam will escape into the air. When possible, use your microwave oven.

2. Use exhaust fans and open vents while cooking washing dishes, or bathing to remove that additional moisture before it mixes with the room air.

3. Keep roof vents cracked slightly all the time. This ventilation will allow the continuous escape of humid air, but the heat loss is minimal.

4. Open a window for five minutes twice a day to replace humid stale air with fresh dry air.

5. Use a mechanical dehumidifier. An inexpensive substitute can be made by placing "kitty litter" in the bottom of cake pans. Set pans on counter tops to help absorb the moisture from the air.

6. Storm windows reduce the contrast in surface temperature of windows and the room air by creating dead air space (insulation) between the two glass surfaces.

RV Maintenance Tips

- With a constantly changing water supply to fill your water tank, it is wise to use a disinfectant. Household bleach is a readily available disinfectant. Ratio: six drops to the gallon for city water and twelve drops to the gallon if it is well water.

- Clean the hose at least monthly. Coil the hose. Pour a pint of household bleach into one end of the coiled hose. Then re-connect the ends of the hose and rotate the coiled hose slowly to allow bleach to clean it. Hook the hose to water and flush.

- Whenever you hook up to a water source, run fresh water through the hose before connecting it to your RV. This will remove any air or any stale water in the hose.

- WD-40 will remove black marks on the outside of the rig. WD-40 is *toxic*, so wear gloves when you are using it.

- Bug and tar remover will remove any black marks on RV skin.

- If you have tape residue marks that won't come off, MEK (available at most Standard Brands paint stores) will remove it. Again, wear rubber gloves when using MEK.

- If you notice a sewer odor in your rig after dumping, try caulking around roof vent. Odors can seep through tiny cracks. If that doesn't help, the vent pipe may be cracked or you may have a crack in the top of your holding tank where it is vented. Because it is on the top of the tank, it does not leak but it may allow odors to filter into the RV. The only way to correct this is to replace the holding tank or tear the wall out to replace a vent pipe.

- To loosen stubborn wheel lug nuts, place a larger pipe (about two-feet long) over lug-wrench or breaker-bar of a socket set and it will give you extra leverage.

- Carry a set of trailer chocks with you. They come in handy for tire changes as well as parking on hills.

- An improper flame on the water heater is often caused by insects laying eggs or building nests in the tube that provides the air-to-gas mixture. Disassemble tube, inspect, and clean.

Getting Your Mail On The Road

Americans believe it is their "right" to receive mail delivered on time to their front door—even when they are continually moving that door. With mail so important, it is strange that so many road-wise full-timer RVers have never learned to handle their mail properly.

The more time that you spend on the road, the more important it becomes. In addition to necessary mail such as bank statements, insurance premium notices, and registration renewals, there are all those new friends with whom you want to keep in touch. How else will you know when you are both in the same area so you can arrange to meet again? And there are the old friends from back home that you don't want to lose contact with.

The problem is that when we don't get a piece of mail, we may never find out about it. The letter gets returned to the sender with an undeliverable notice. Sometimes it has been forwarded to several addresses before it is sent back. If the original address was to someone who acts as a mail forwarder, all the sender has to do is put it in another envelope and send it back to that same address again. But usually the sender doesn't know that; chances are he never tries to send it again.

Sometimes even when you are actually at the address, a trailer park employee doesn't recognize a variation of your name and may return mail to the sender as undeliverable. If mail arrives after you've moved on, there is a good chance it will be returned to the sender (your mail service). Without a mail service, you might never know that a letter did *not* reach you.

Unless people receive very little mail and have a willing relative who understands all the facets of mail forwarding, we believe that those who RV extensively should use one of the mail forwarding services. (See addresses.) The amount of money that you pay for a good mail service is insignificant compared to knowing that *all* your mail will reach you. With a mail service, you know you'll get your mail regardless of weather, vacations, or emergencies.

Mail Forwarding Services

There are three types of forwarding services. Providers of the first two are listed in the yellow pages under addresses in the back of this book. The third type is listed in the yellow pages of your local telephone directory.

1. **Free forwarding services:** Some clubs forward mail free as part of their service to members. It takes too many working hours for most large organizations to assume this responsibility without compensation, so their forwarding procedure is limited by strict rules.

   There are a few small clubs who forward for members who are on vacation, but if the volume of mail is heavy or if it continues over a long period of time, they may ask the member to subscribe to a commercial system. Remember, that somebody is donating their time or everyone is sharing the cost for one person's benefit.

2. **Commercial services** designed for travelers are the fairest method and provide a broader range of forwarding services. They have a trained staff who understand how to provide the most efficient service. They band the individual letters into tear-proof envelopes or priority mail holders that assure that the outer envelope won't fall apart in postal handling. All commercial services are required by law to affix new postage to the outer envelope.

3. **Private mail box companies** were designed for local businesses or for privacy and security of handling mail. Their charge is higher, but most of these companies will forward mail for traveling customers and will do it efficiently.

Some mail services also have a message service for an additional fee. Remember, a message service, whether strictly an answering service or an electronic voice message service, is of no benefit unless the subscribers call in on a regular schedule to get the messages that were left for them.

Giving Mail Forwarding Instructions

1. Have your forwarder repackage your mail, putting all the envelopes inside one large, tear-proof envelope. The forwarder's return address is on this tear-proof envelope so that, if the mail misses you for any reason, it will be returned to the forwarder (not the people who wrote the letters). The forwarder can then forward it to your next address.

2. Be sure that you give an exact date to start forwarding to a specific address and the date to stop sending to that address.

3. Don't give too many instructions at one time. Planning too far ahead limits your travels and confuses the forwarder. It's better to send frequent changes through telephone calls than to give a long detailed itinerary that covers several weeks.

4. If there is a chance that you won't be at the RV park office or post office on the date the mail is to arrive, have your forwarder write *"hold for arrival"* on the front of the envelope to prevent someone sending it back before you arrive to claim it.

5. If you are using General Delivery for a pickup point, select a small town post office not one in a big city.

6. If you've been receiving mail at one address, have your forwarder write *"last mail to this address"* on the last envelope so that you will know when you receive the last packet.

7. If the forwarder has so much mail that it won't fit into a single envelope, have her write on the corner of each envelope *one of two, and two of two* etc. so you'll know if you have *all* the mail. Even though mail is sent from the exact same post office at the exact same time, letters don't always arrive at the same time. You could receive one envelope full of mail and think you have it all and then move on never knowing there was one or more envelopes that you didn't receive.

8. Be sure your forwarder has an accurate scale to determine proper postage instead of guessing at the amount. Otherwise you'll either pay more postage than is required or you'll have to make a special trip to the post office to pay additional charges.

Ordering Goods By Mail/Telephone

Many RVers shop by mail/phone because the products needed come from specialty RV stores or directly from a manufacturer. The problem is we can't always tell if the merchandise is what a catalog promises them to be. It can be frustrating if the delivery is late when we are itching to go on down the road.

The Federal Trade Commission's *"Mail Order Rules"* give some protection on the latter problem because they require mail-order companies to send ordered goods within the time period stated in their catalog or ad. If the company can't ship on time, it is required to notify you and to provide a postage-paid notice allowing you to cancel—for a full refund if the new shipping date is not acceptable. This applies to everything you order by mail or by telephone except cash-on-delivery orders.

If you don't receive the goods, or have any problem with the way the order was filled, or with its condition on arrival, call the company and explain the problem. Follow the telephone call with a letter outlining your understanding of the telephone communication and how the company promised to correct it.

If they do not carry out their agreement to rectify within 30 days (or a specified time period), notify them by mail or phone that if satisfaction is not received within the next ten days you will notify such agencies as Direct Marketing Association, the Better Business Bureau, and the U.S. Postal Service. Usually the threat of a complaint to these agencies brings quick results.

Direct Marketing Association has a "Mail Order Action Line" that will intervene with companies for you. It also maintains a "Mail Preference Service" where you can write to ask to have your name added to or removed from telephone sales lists. (See addresses.)

The Council of Better Business Bureaus (BBB) will tell you who to call to register a complaint. Your complaint must be registered at the BBB office nearest to the *company's headquarters*.

Send the U.S. Postal Service, Chief Postal Inspector, a copy of your complaint letter and all documentation.

Hints on Ordering By Mail

1. Check the company's return policy in case the merchandise does not meet your expectations. Some companies guarantee to refund your money in full if you are not completely satisfied and will so state in their advertisement. Deal with those companies whenever you can. Most companies do have a time limit of 10 to 30 days after delivery in which you can request a refund. Many do not strictly enforce that date as they want to satisfy you so you'll become a repeat customer.

2. In comparing costs of companies that offer the same merchandise, look at any extra costs. Some companies include the shipping charge in the stated price and others add it on either as a flat fee or a fee based on cost and weight. Remember to figure in the sales tax. You should be exempt from paying it for out-of-state mail orders *unless* the company has another facility in the state you are ordering from. A few states have a law requiring taxes be paid even if merchandise comes from out of state. RV travelers should avoid ordering while in those states.

3. Fill out the provided order form as completely as possible. Use their form, not just a letter, because you may omit important details and because their employees are trained to follow the company's order forms.

4. Keep a copy of the order form with the company's name, phone number, catalog number, and your check number. Plan to be at the address you've given them before the expected date of arrival. Notify the park to hold your packages until your arrive.

5. You get faster service if you pay by credit card as many companies will not fill an order until the check has time to clear.

6. If you order by telephone, you definitely should have the merchandise charged to your credit card or the order will be sent C.O.D. Remember, you pay extra for C.O.D. orders.

7. If a company offers an optional insurance fee to cover loss or damage in transportation, don't agree to it! It is the shipper's responsibility to make sure the merchandise arrives safely and on time.

How Much Does It Cost to Full-time?

How much it costs to live in an RV depends on what you do. If you stay in commercial parks at a nightly rate of $10 to $20, your "rent" will be $300 to $600 a month. If you use freebies, you'll pay no rent at all. Our newly revised book, *Survival of the RV Snowbirds,* shows you how to live rent-free all year if necessary.

Many RVers use freebies while traveling and stay in parks with amenities when they "sit." A park with a swimming pool, will average between $225 and $325 rental on a monthly basis. During the prime snowbird and tourist seasons, especially in Arizona, California, and Florida those figures will double.

Parking fees are the best place to cut back if your budget gets out of hand. Many RVers buy a membership in a "home" park that allows them to participate in the Camp Coast to Coast system. There are also the free (or almost free) "coyote" campgrounds, such as the BLM land known as Senator Wash on the southern Arizona/California border.

Food is another variable. If you buy specials and eat all your meals at home, your monthly food bill will be smaller than ours because we eat out a great deal. Our food bill is less than our neighbor, even though they eat out as much as we do, because we go to chains like Golden Corral or Sizzler while they patronize gourmet restaurants.

A general guide is how much do you spend on food now? It will be about the same. That's true of medical, too. You will probably spend only half as much on entertainment as the house-liver because RVers have more opportunities for free entertainment. You should also spend less than half as much on clothes because you don't have room for them and because being in style loses its importance.

Gasoline is higher at first because of the tendency to "see it all" at a vacationer's fast pace. When you taper down to a slower pace, gasoline may be even *less* than when you lived in a house, driving two vehicles.

We know RVers who are living on less than $800 or $900 a month. We know others who say they could not get by on less than $2,500 a month. However, the majority of RVers seem to be living happily on $1200 to $1700 a month

Supplementing Your Pension

If you don't have enough money to full-time the way that you desire, don't give up full-timing. Instead, supplement your income with one of the hundreds of temporary, seasonal, and "consulting" opportunities that are available on a short-term basis.

One popular way is by working in sales. There are always opportunities for working seasonal sales jobs at places like the Hamilton Stores at the National Parks.

Many RVers work for companies that need traveling sales people. One of the best such jobs is selling ads for campground giveaway maps. The two biggest employers are American Guide Services (out of Washington) and Southeast Publications (out of Florida). Both companies produce high-quality campground maps. This job is especially satisfying to full-time RVers because they can continue to travel. Each sales person (or couple) selects the part of the country where they want to work, and they can select how much time they want to devote to selling ads.

Camping World, a nationwide chain of RV accessory stores, also hires part-time sales people as well as service technicians and cashiers during their busy season in various locations. This is a job opportunity for any RVers who want to put their RVing knowledge to work.

The corporation address is in Bowling Green, Kentucky. Some of the Camping World stores that normally hire seasonally are found in Garland, Texas, Kissimmee, Florida, Myrtle Beach, South Carolina, and Phoenix, Arizona.

You will also find there are opportunities for new and challenging jobs in local newspapers. Most start at minimum wage, so the competition is less. There are also several newsletters for RVers who are looking for unique opportunities.

See addresses for temp jobs.

Applying For a Temporary Job

Applying for a temporary job has some differences. Full-timers with backgrounds in medicine, dentistry, and similar professions that require a state license find that it isn't worth the cost and hassle to try to work part time in more than one state. Knowing that vacation relief is much needed, and usually having contacts in the area from which they retired, they return for short periods of work.

This same concept can apply to any career. If you are looking for a temporary job in drafting, management, any type of office work, or in any specialized area, you will need a resume.

Writing a resume

If you don't know how to write a resume, borrow a how-to book from the library. Be sure your resume looks, as well as sounds, good. It must be typed. If you don't have a typewriter, most public libraries have one that you can use. Misspelled words and bad grammar count against you, so if these are areas where you don't do well, consider going to a typing service (listed in phone book) and have one done for you. Just write down the basic facts and let the typist put it together. Keep it to one page if possible, and avoid long, rambling details.

Don't include jobs that you held for just a brief period unless they have a direct bearing on the present job. Lots of employment changes look bad. Don't advertise your transient life. Leave that for the interview after you have won the employer's interest.

Interviewing for a temporary job

Be careful what you say in that social chitchat which may take place before or after the formal interview. Don't be afraid to talk during the interview, but listen too. Be assertive, but not aggressive. Ask questions about the job. And don't let the interview end until you've had a chance to sell yourself.

Chances are you will be overqualified for most temporary jobs that are available. You might not want to disclose all of your qualifications because the employer may not want to hire you if he realizes you won't stay with the job. Under some circumstances, this may also be the time to be candid.

Point out the advantages of hiring you as a consultant or a short-term employee—advantages such as not having to pay you the benefits other employees receive like sick days, holidays and vacations.

Don't raise the salary question until after you've given a complete summary of your assets and have explained how you expect to contribute to this company. Don't be overly concerned with a small salary. You can afford to get less money in salary and fringe benefits because it costs you less to live, and because you are looking for an interim job, not a lifetime position. This gives you an advantage over other applicants.

If you are not qualified but really want the job, offer to train without pay for a week. Chances are the employer will pay you anyway, but your offer is impressive. If you end up working for a week without pay, you'll at least have gained knowledge that you can use next time.

After you get the job

Make friends with the staff. One way to do this is to alleviate anyone's fears that you are out to get their job. Knowing you are not competing with them can turn potential enemies into friends and thus make your work days more enjoyable.

Learn what is expected of you, and don't be afraid to ask questions. Always do the best work that you can just because it is more satisfying. If you have to work, you might as well enjoy it.

When a job becomes boring or there is too much pressure, it is time to move on. Leave the headache pills and ulcer soothers for those who have no choice but to stick with the job. Go on down the road. There is another job in the next place you stop—or the one after that.

Volunteer Campground Host Program

One of the most appealing jobs to full-time RVers isn't really a job at all. It is a mutual-benefit exchange. You *volunteer* your services for a few hours each day for a free parking place.

The big advantage to being a volunteer campground host is that you can work where, when, and for whom you wish. The Bureau of Land Management (BLM) uses some campground hosts. The Forest Service (FS) uses many volunteer hosts for both short term and for an entire season. The Corps of Engineers (COE) auctions its jobs to the lowest bidder for fee-collecting and hosting. The National Park Service has all kinds of opportunities. Their *"Volunteers In the Parks"* program depends on the specific needs and on the budgets at each separate park. And many of the states also have volunteer host programs.

Once you have worked in any volunteer project, that experience helps you to get into the next program. Many people find a "dream job" and return to it year after year, while others prefer to go to a different place each summer. A few people work one job in the summer, and then they go to another one for the winter.

Generally, volunteers get a free camping spot with partial hookups. In exchange, the volunteer does the little things that without him would go undone. Learn in advance what is expected so you won't take on a job that is too much for your physical abilities. There are many degrees of job requirements, so select one you'll be able to stay with for your contract period.

Nancy Bedford Jones said, "The volunteering road may not be the most traveled one, but it is an artery of major importance that can take us places no other road goes. Like all roads, it has both smooth and rough places, with an occasional pothole and detours, or even a dead end. It also has joyous arrivals at friendships, usefulness, and learning, as well as an unending list of personal rewards. Like the freeways we all travel, it is a challenge to make of the experience whatever we want to make it."

See index for National Park Service addresses and look under Temporary Job Opportunities in the back of this book.

Getting Cash As You Travel

Many travelers use credit cards, but there are times when a credit card is not accepted or when using it means paying a higher price. For example, you may save up to ten cents a gallon for gasoline by paying cash.

There are many different ways to handle cash and each has its supporters. One couple carry a thousand dollars in cash with them. When they reach their seasonal destination, they deposit the cash in a *savings* account in a local bank. This credit base allows them to cash checks from their home bank for up to the thousand dollar "security." By putting cash into a savings account there is no time delay for the check to clear. They earn interest on the money between travels. When they are ready to leave, they close the savings account and take the cash to the next town.

Traveler's Checks are expensive to use and many businesses will not accept them in payment any more readily than a personal check. You may have to cash them at a bank.

Certified Checks are also difficult to cash in many places because they are easy to forge. Businesses and banks may not cash them even if you have identification.

Money market funds: If you prefer to have your money earning interest while still being available to you, consider a money market fund (MMF). Minimum deposit and minimum amount you write checks for will vary from company to company, so check several for the one that best suits your needs.

Most full-timers use the checks to transfer their money from the MMF to an ATM account from which they can make withdrawals as needed. Each check you write must be $500 or more. Most banks, other than the one where your MMF is located, will cash $500 MMF checks for you.

The other type of MMF is a cash management account (CMA) which requires a larger initial investment, but once that initial deposit is made, you can let your balance fall to whatever you wish. Most Money Market Funds pay a higher rate of interest than do savings accounts, and have the added advantage of issuing a debit/credit card.

Automatic Teller Machines (ATM)

Many banks now belong to one of two nationwide automatic teller machine (ATM) systems—PLUS or CIRRUS. These automatic teller machines are open 24 hours a day and seven days a week, thus solving the full-timer's problem of getting access to his own funds.

Travelers can use the automatic teller machine system for most banking transactions, including obtaining $100 or more cash per day. CIRRUS, for example, has over 10,000 locations across the United States and Canada where you can use their network. CIRRUS automatic teller machines can be found in over 2,600 cities and are in all but four states—and those four states may be added by the time this book is printed.

To use either the PLUS or the CIRRUS's automatic teller machine systems, you simply get a special card from your bank that allows you to key into the automatic teller machine at any affiliated bank. You receive a directory of where to find these affiliated banks when you get your card. In addition to a directory of locations, both systems have toll-free numbers which you can call to find the nearest automatic teller machine.

The instructions for using the automatic teller machine card are printed on each machine. It is a sophisticated system which even tells you when you've made a mistake. ATM cards make an immediate transfer to or from your savings or checking accounts, so be sure to add it to your record.

Warning: If the machine rejects your request, better try another machine or wait until the bank is open as these machines have been known to "eat" cards when there is any problem.

Telephone Bill Paying (TBP) is a similar system which will, on your touch tone telephonic command, pay those creditors you have previously identified with assigned numbers. You punch in the numbers which identify your account, the creditor, the date to be paid, and the amount. Record these transactions in your checkbook register, too.

Using Credit/Debit Cards

Because merchants are unwilling to accept out-of-state checks, you do need some type of credit card. *Credit* cards, such as Master Card and Visa, permit periodic payments of less than the full balance, and add an interest charge each month if there is an unpaid balance. The credit system allows you to examine the bill before paying it.

Debit/credit cards are not truly a credit card because the transaction is immediately deducted from your account. Record it in your account register just as if you had written a check. Many people feel the debit/credit card is better because, with the money being withdrawn from your account, you don't have to worry about billing reaching you in time. You don't pay any interest or credit card fees.

With a debit/credit card, there are no fees such as a credit card would charge if you got a cash advance. Nor is there a maximum limit that you can get. You can withdraw any amount up to the balance of your account. You do receive a monthly statement that shows all checks and debit transactions.

You need to shop for the best bank credit card because all have different interest rates and service charges. That is because each bank can set its own interest rates and annual fees as long as it stays below the maximum allowed.

For instance, if you spend $500 a month with a credit card and you use the revolving credit feature, 19.8% interest can cost you about $480 a year. If you get a card that charges 12%, your credit-card costs would be closer to $300 a year, a savings of $180. So unless you habitually pay off your credit card charge each month, you need to find a bank that charges a low interest rate.

But if you do pay the balance each month, the interest rate is not important. You need to look for an issuer who doesn't charge an annual fee. It is important to know that a card with no annual fee is not always a *free* card. Some banks charge an "access transaction" or "usage fee" every time a card is used even though you pay it off in full when the bill comes in.

Remember, you don't have to get a credit card from the bank where your money is deposited! Many banks across the country will process applications nationwide.

Bankcard Holders of America has a list of about two dozen banks around the country that do not charge any annual fee for their card. It also has a list of about 30 banks that charge reduced interest rates as low as 16.5%. The cost of the first list is $1.95 and only $1.00 for the second list: Bankcard Holders of America, 333 Pennsylvania Avenue SE, Washington, DC 20003.

Selecting a Bank

You should shop for the best home bank. This does not mean you must find a bank in the same town as your former--or present--home base. You can select a bank in any of the 50 states and do all your banking by mail.

The First Interstate Bank is preferred by many RVers who spend time primarily in the western states because it has over 1000 offices in more than 18 states and is affiliated with the CIRRUS automatic teller network. Any of the First Interstate banks can be used by the traveler as if it were the home bank. All you need is a check guarantee (gold) card from your home bank. With it, you can cash a personal check for any amount or withdraw all your funds just as if you were at your home bank.

Check the banks as you travel until you find the one that gives you the best services. Travelers need one that is affiliated with the CIRRUS or the PLUS networks.

Special Services

Some banks offer special services, such as free checking to those over 65, free travelers checks, or a telephone bill paying service through which you can pay monthly bills with a single telephone call. For instance, Pacific First Federal in Tacoma, Washington, gives free TBP (if you maintain a minimum balance in your checking account) and even provides an 800 number for in- and out-of-state calls.

Shop until you find a bank that gives the services you want.

Renting or Buying a Used RV

If you buy a new RV, the dealer will spend time showing you how the systems work and will usually give you an instruction book. When you buy a used unit, especially one that is sold on consignment, or when you rent a unit, you may only get a cursory briefing. Insist on getting complete instructions.

1. Have the agent or seller show you how all the hookups work, including water, septic system, and electric. Ask him to stand by while you run through the procedure yourself to make certain you understand how it works.

2. Before you sign the contract, have the agent accompany you on a test drive both on and off the premises. You do the driving. The agent is there for instruction only.

3. If you are renting, ask how any breakdowns are to be handled. Be sure you have adequate collision and liability insurance. Find out if there is a deductible that you have to pay before the insurance takes over.

4. Whether renting or buying a used vehicle, read the contract through at least twice and don't let anyone hurry you through the readings. You need to know exactly what you are responsible for. Don't take the agent's word that anything that isn't to your satisfaction will be added later. Promises can be misunderstood or broken. The agent/seller is only held accountable by law for what is actually in the written contract at the time of signing.

5. Note: If you buy a used unit—especially one that is sold on consignment—do not hand over the check until you see the signed title. Sadly, friends of ours lost $10,000 to a dealer who was "such a nice guy." They accepted his explanation as to why he did not have the title yet and agreed to let him mail it to them "in a few days." It turned out that the bank owned the truck and the "nice guy' had been running a scam for many months. Buyers gave him their checks, but he never paid the bank, so the people never got their titles. He was caught; the bank took the vehicles back, but our friends and several other buyers lost the money they had paid.

Medical Emergencies on the Road

Have you ever thought about what you would do if your spouse had a heart attack or stroke while driving your rig? If the driver has medical problems such as heart trouble, high blood pressure, diabetes, or any type of illness where a sudden attack can take place, it is important to think about what you should do. In the event of a sudden loss of consciousness, the driver's leg could stiffen and push on the accelerator.

The first rule is: Don't panic! Try to get between the driver and the steering wheel so you can steer the vehicle off the roadway. If you cannot push the driver's foot off the accelerator and apply the brake, turn the key off to stop the motor.

Vehicles with power steering lose that power when the key is turned off, but in most cases you can steer as long as the vehicle has momentum.

If you are towing a trailer on a downgrade where the vehicle continues to gain momentum, and you cannot stop it with the foot brake, reach for the trailer's hand brake control and apply all the pressure you can with one hand while you steer with the other.

Once you have brought the vehicles to a stop, check to see if the victim is still breathing. If not, pull the victim to the ground off the roadway but where you can be seen by passing vehicles. If you are unable to administer CPR or artificial respiration, get on the CB and call for help, or go to the roadway and signal passing motorists to stop. Many RVers carry a "HELP NEEDED" sign that they can place in a window to solicit aid.

It is highly unlikely that this situation will occur. In most cases, a heart attack or stroke victim has enough warning to get off the roadway. But if you have thought ahead about what to do, you're less likely to panic and do the wrong thing.

If your spouse is a known candidate for heart attack or stroke, make it your business to learn the proper emergency care. Many organizations provide free CPA courses. Check with the chamber of commerce or Red Cross to find out when and where the next course that is convenient for you will take place.

Medical Records

Illness can happen without any warning. When it does, we seem to expect the new doctor—who has never seen us before—to make a correct diagnosis. Yet, what do we tell him? "I have something wrong with my heart, but I don't know what it is. I take a little white pill every day. I can't remember the name."

Or perhaps, "My doctor lives in Oregon. He said to call any time day or night." The truth is you can't even be sure of reaching your former doctor during office hours. If you did reach him at home, do you really think he will remember you—let alone be able to recite your record from memory?

To avoid the expense and delay of repeat tests:

1. Be knowledgeable about your health, good or bad. Don't rely on your spouse to know it all. Know what medications you take and what they are for. And know your allergies and diseases.

2. Write the above on a card and *both* partners carry copies of it.

3. Keep a copy of the above information in a "vial of life" (plastic container) stored in your refrigerator. When paramedics see the alert decal on your door, they know to look for it. Check with local paramedics to learn where to obtain the vial of life.

4. Wear a medication allergy bracelet. Emergency people, responding to an accident call, do not have time to search purses or look for wallets, but they do check for allergy bracelets.

5. Join one of the several companies, such as Med Report, that give 24-hour immediate access to all your medical records.

6. Obtain a synopsis of your last medical checkup (EKG, lab work, X-rays). Busy emergency room doctors do not have time to wade through pages of history.

The 1970 "Patient's Bill of Rights" law requires that doctors and hospitals must give patients access to their own medical records. Some charge money per page for this information, but you only need the discharge summary, copies of tests taken, and treatment given.

Getting Prescriptions Filled

The best way for travelers to get medicine is through one of the mail order drug companies because these companies are able to fill prescriptions regardless of where the prescribing doctor is licensed. Refills are equally easy to obtain through mail order pharmacies. Narcotics are the only drugs that you cannot get through mail order.

When a doctor orders a new medicine, we request that it be written in two separate prescriptions. One is for a two-week supply to be filled at the local drug store for immediate use. The second prescription is for the remainder (with refill capabilities). This one we send to our mail order pharmacy who fills and mails it by first class mail to whatever address we request. When we are ready for a refill we write or call the company and they send it immediately. This eliminates any problem with a pharmacist being unable to fill a prescription that was written by a doctor who is registered to practice in a different state.

A list of mail order pharmacies is in the address section. However, with today's computer capabilities, some drugstore chains (such as Walgreen) can now give refills as you travel. Take the initial prescription to the chain pharmacy closest to the doctor. Make sure they have out-of-state refill capabilities via a computer system. Then when you need a refill in another state, you simply go to the same drugstore chain and get your refill. If there are no more refills, the initial pharmacist can call the doctor and possibly get a refill.

We try to remember to ask the doctor to give us the generic name of the prescribed drug. If we forget, most mail order pharmacies will give the generic equivalent if you request it. A generic equivalent costs considerably less than a brand drug.

When we buy Tylenol, aspirin, and similar over-the-counter drugs, we look for generic equivalents. The store brand is usually setting right beside the brand name drug. Read the ingredients on both packages and you will see they are identical. Why pay extra money just for the name?

See Addresses for list of mail order pharmacies.

Generic Drugs

The American Association of Retired Persons (AARP) has been fighting for a national repeal of the anti-generic substitution laws. Most states now allow a substitution of generic at your request, even if the doctor didn't write the prescription that way. However, most doctors will prescribe a generic equivalent if you ask them.

It is understandable that pharmaceutical companies fight against generic substitutions. They are trying to convince physicians (and customers) that the generic drugs are not as safe, or as effective, as their higher-priced brand-name products. It leaves you wondering what the truth is when you hear physicians and educators on TV talking against generic drugs.

In a 1987 report, AARP stated that "A number of these 'experts' are being paid by the brand drug companies whose products are threatened by generic competition."

Whether that is true or not, the fact is that all drugs—generic or brand name—must meet the same standards of purity, strength, and quality. These standards are set and enforced by the U.S. Food & Drug Administration. Generic drug manufacturers must also show that their product behaves in the same way that the brand name product does.

Generic drugs do not look like their brand name components. They may be a different color or shape. That is not important. What is important is that the generic drugs often cost about half what their brand name components cost.

This includes many over-the-counter drugs, too. Read the labels on products such as Tylenol (by McNeil Laboratories) and K-Nol, a generic substitution put out by K-Mart. They are identical except for price.

If you want to save money, start reading the labels instead of just picking up the familiar brand name.

RV Insurance

Full-time RVers have fewer insurance options than most people in our society. Full-timers may have a perfect driving record, yet most companies will not insure us if the company knows we live full time in our RV. This is because they have no statistics on which to base our accident history. They think of us as getting behind a wheel and driving endless hours the way vacationers so often do.

An agent may never before have met anyone who lives full-time in an RV, so he doesn't really know management's policy on it. He may assure you that living full time in the RV is no problem because he can find nothing in the literature addressing it. All is fine—until you are involved in an accident. If it then comes out that you live full time in the RV, the company can refuse to pay the claim. If they do pay the claim, based on proof that your agent was advised about your lifestyle, chances are your insurance will be cancelled afterwards, leaving you to find new insurance at a time when your accident record makes it most difficult.

The following companies are the only ones we know of that will write special insurance for RVers and who have stated they will cover full-time RVers. (See addresses under insurance.)

* Alexander & Alexander: motor homes only.
* Caravanner Insurance: trailers only.
* Foremost Insurance: motor homes and trailers.
* Minnehoma Insurance: trailers only.
* National General: all types.
* Progressive Insurance: all types (in most states).

Foremost offers a special policy for trailers that are parked for long periods. When you want to move the trailer, you must notify them and pay an additional premium for the travel days.

Minnehoma and Caravanner are generally less expensive because they cover only travel trailers. You must get your tow vehicle insured elsewhere. This isn't a problem because any insurance company will cover the tow vehicle since you do not live in it full time.

Foremost insures both trailers and motor homes, but except in a few states, it doesn't cover towing or towed vehicles.

Personal Liability Coverage

RVers who still have a house are covered for personal liability under their home owner's policy, no matter where they go. But those who sell their house to live and travel full time in an RV have had, until recently, no good way to get *personal* liability.

Full-timers have known that, but didn't worry about it until ridiculous law suits became the style. Now it is a serious concern to some of them.

Most specialized RV insurance companies have what is called *campsite liability coverage*—coverage inside your RV and on the immediate site where the RV is parked. So, if someone who is visiting you falls going out the door, gets hurt and sues, you are covered. The same is true if someone trips on a water hose stretched across your parking site.

Campsite liability coverage does not cover accidents which are your fault when you are away from the RV. For example, you are playing golf and your ball hits someone in the eye. A homeowner policy would cover that personal liability, but the policies available to full-time RVers would not.

Foremost and National General Insurance now have personal liability protection packages for full-timers that also include medical payments, emergency first aid to others, and personal effects. However, there are some states where this coverage isn't available. Check into it if personal liability is a concern to you while away from your RV.

Most companies settle claims quickly and fairly.

To change insurance companies, you must have a clean driving record—no accidents or outstanding traffic tickets within the past three to five years.

The Importance of a Will

When you die, will the things you leave behind go to the people you want to receive them? If you die without a will, the state steps in and decides who gets your assets. Don't fool yourself into thinking that it doesn't matter because you intend to spend all your money before you die. There is life insurance, the RV and other vehicles, personal items, a nest egg, etc.

If there is no will, your assets are divided by a mathematical formula. The state also decides who will administer your estate and how much that person will be paid. All costs—including court costs and lawyer's fees—will come out of your estate.

In a community property state (e.g. Texas), if you die without a will, half of the community property goes to your children (including stepchildren) or to the children of children. Your surviving spouse receives *nothing!* The surviving spouse may get the "right to use" one-third of your real property during his or her lifetime, after which the property reverts back to the children in its entirety. If that is *not* how you wish to distribute your assets, you must have a will and it must be one that suffices to pass on your property according to your state's laws.

Find a qualified attorney in the state where you have a home base to write a will for you.

The living bank

With so many people needing the gift of an organ—a kidney, heart, liver—consider becoming an organ donor.

1. Register with "The Living Bank"—a national contact registry for organs. There is no charge to get your name in the registry, although donations are welcome to offset costs of maintaining the registry.

2. Make sure that your doctor and family are aware of your desire. Call 1-800-528-2971.

3. If you do not want to be kept alive by heroic measures, make a "Living Will" by writing out a statement to that effect. Give one copy to your doctor, one to your family, and keep one with your insurance papers.

Handling Important Records

Review your records annually and discard those that are outdated or no longer of value. This includes checks and bills that can't be used for tax purposes. Put all the important, original documents in a safe deposit box. Give a key to someone you trust so that you can obtain the original if you are out-of-state.

Records that should be kept in a safe deposit box are a list of important contacts such as attorneys, doctors, bankers, creditors and debtors; birth, marriage, and stock certificates; divorce and other legal papers; service and citizenship records; deeds to property you own; and the *original* "last will and testament." (Copies are fine for reference, but are not legal documents.) Also, include an inventory of the primary possessions you take with you, with the worth of each, in case of fire or theft. Make a notation of what you want done with each of these possessions if you should die.

Take copies of all of the above with you.

The next step is to set up a filing system that will make it easy to find the records when you need them. We suggest buying two plastic file boxes of different colors. One color will be to keep all active records in and the other for inactive records. You also need a package of file folders. That way you can separate papers into labeled file folders for easy retrieval.

Your active file box could hold unpaid bills, current receipts, bank statements, cancelled checks, and income tax papers. At the end of the year, you would move these to the inactive file box.

Items which should always remain in your active file box are current bills, employment records, health policies, credit card information including the number of each credit card, insurance policies, copy of will, appliance manuals and warranties, Social Security information, and a list of everything that is in the safe deposit box, with name of the bank and its location. Include a safe deposit key or combination, too.

Make sure your spouse knows where the records are kept, including regular bills to be paid. You should also tell whomever is going to handle the estate where to find this information.

Changing Your Residency

Accountants and lawyers advise those who are changing their state of residency to take all "property" with you. If you leave some assets in the former state, and change your residence to another, your heirs may have to pay *two* inheritance taxes—one to each of the states involved.

All states hate to lose taxpayers, so when you die you can be sure the former state is going to try to collect taxes from your estate if there is any loophole that will allow it to do so. For this reason, you are advised to cut your ties with the former state.

Cutting Former State Ties

1. File an Affidavit of Domicile in the new state where you wish to be a resident.

2. Send a copy of this Affidavit of Domicile to the tax department of the former state and to the place where you formerly voted and ask them to remove your name from the voting register.

3. Register to vote in the new state.

4. Register vehicles in new state and get a driver's license.

5. Move all property on which a tax can be levied— stocks, bonds, mortgages, bank accounts, notes etc. to the new state. When you move your residence, bring as much as you can of your property with you.

It is not our intention to give legal advice, but because this is an important consideration for those who are starting full-time RVing, or for those who reside in one state part of the year, have vehicles registered in another, and a bank account or property in yet another, we asked two attorneys their opinion.

Both confirmed that, generally, personal property passes according to the laws of the jurisdiction of the domicile of the decedent. If more than one state can make this claim, the estate would have to pay "death" taxes to all involved. At the least it would mean a lengthy and costly legal battle.

When you decide where you want your residence to be, find an attorney who has experience in probate and have him draw up new wills.

Fire Extinguishers

There are three classes of fire. Class A, the most common, involves combustible material—paper, wood, fabrics, and some plastics. For this type, you need at least one 5-pound "A" or "A:B:C" extinguisher. RV fires spread rapidly, and once out of control, the battle is lost. Too small an extinguisher is as bad as none at all. However, poisonous fumes from burning plastics often keep one from getting close enough to adequately fight a class A fire except in its earliest stage.

Dry chemical extinguishers are the most effective, least toxic, and least expensive. If you have to use one, you'll have a mess to clean up afterwards. Be sure that the extinguisher label says it is rated for "A" as well as "B:C" fires.

RVers are advised to buy an extinguisher in an all-metal container. Cheaper types sold in discount stores usually have plastic heads and containers that may not withstand the vibrations of rough roads. You'll pay more, but buying through a reputable dealer means help in selection and a demonstration on how to use it. (See yellow pages in local telephone book.)

Halon extinguishers are excellent fire fighters but are expensive and many people are afraid of them because they've heard halon is poisonous. Halon is not dangerous if handled properly. The Air Force uses halon almost exclusively on its flight lines.

You can purchase Halon extinguishers at RV supply stores or through extinguisher dealers. A 2-1/2 pound bottle (rated for B & C fires) costs about $75. This, and the 5 lb.. size, are rated only for Class B (propane, gasoline, oil) and Class C (electrical) fires. What you really need is the 9 pound halon extinguisher which is rated for all three types—A:B:C- fires. It sells for around $125.

Before you decide it is too expensive, remember that you can often buy it at a discount, and the halon extinguisher (unlike chemical types) can be used effectively as long as there is any fluid left. Using it once doesn't mean it must be recharged (even if the gauge shows "recharge"). Recharging is expensive— about $10 a pound.

Smoke Alarms

Smoke alarms are considered essential for nighttime use in RVs because of the toxic fumes from burning plastics, Formica, and formaldehyde and the fact that an RV burns so quickly once a fire gets started. There are two types of smoke alarms:

(1) Photoelectric which contain a small light source and a photocell. When smoke enters the detector, light is reflected from smoke particles into the photocell and the alarm is triggered.

(2) Ionization chamber detector contains a small radiation source that produces electrically charged air molecules called ions. The presence of these ions allows a small electric current to flow into the chamber. When smoke particles enter the chamber, they attach themselves to these ions, reducing the flow of electric current. The change in the current sets off the alarm.

Both types are equally effective. The ionization detector will respond more quickly to flaming fires while photoelectric detectors respond faster to smoldering fires. Make certain the detector you buy has been approved by a major testing laboratory such as UL (Underwriters Laboratories, Inc.).

In an RV, the detector should be as near as possible to the sleeping area and as far as possible from the kitchen since cooking smoke can cause frequent and annoying false alarms. You may still have to cover the smoke detector when you are frying or making toast because it is so sensitive. The method we recommend is to cover the alarm by slipping a shower cap over it. Sew or pin a brightly colored ribbon to the shower cap so it will hang down in the passageway. This will remind you to uncover the detector after you eat. Another way is to take the detector down and place it under your pillow during daytime.

Remember that when your smoke detector is dismantled, it is valueless.

When you buy an RV smoke detector, make sure it is battery-powered so that it will work whether you are hooked to city power or using your own self-containment. Replace the batteries annually, or sooner if it is necessary.

Making Your RV Flame-Resistant

There are fire-retardant and "flameproof" solutions on the market that you can apply to curtains, carpets, upholstery, unfinished lumber, and just about anything porous enough to absorb it. It takes about a quart per 100 square feet, and every time the material is washed new solution must be applied. At $20 per quart, this becomes expensive.

Instead of buying commercial products, you can make your own fire-retardant and flame-proofing solutions. Farmer's Bulletin #1786: *Fireproofing Fabrics*, published by the U.S. Department of Agriculture Research Service, gives these formulas:

(1) For "wash-and-wear" garments and all fabrics *except* rayon or resin-treated cotton: **7 oz. Borax/3 oz. boric acid/2 quarts hot water.** Dissolve boric acid by making a paste with a small quantity of the water. Add this and the Borax to water. Stir until solution is clear. Warm solution again if it becomes cloudy or jellied from standing. Fabrics treated with this solution do not flame when exposed to fire. Stored materials may lose their flame resistance in time. Repeat treatment annually.

(2) For resin-treated cotton or rayon fabrics: **12 oz. diammonium phosphate/2 quarts water**. Add chemicals to water and stir until solution is clear. This is less flame-retardant than #1, but has good glow-retardant properties. It has a greater tendency to weaken fabrics that are stored for long periods.

NOTE: You can iron treated fabrics whether they were dipped, sprayed, or sprinkled. After applying the solution, allow the fabrics to nearly dry before ironing. Do *not* re-dampen with water. Use a moderately hot iron. If the fabric is wet, or the iron is too hot, the solution will stick to the iron. If this happens, wipe iron with a damp cloth.

These solutions cause a slight stiffening of the fabric, but cause no appreciable change in the feel or color of the material. Treated garments should not irritate skin. You can purchase the chemicals at grocery and drug stores—you don't need pharmaceutical grades.

Tips On Fire-Prevention

- Studies by the Center for Auto Safety show that the LP gas system in RVs can be a fire hazard due to fittings coming loose when traveling over rough roads. The best insurance against this is a propane leak detector and/or periodic checking of your LP system, especially after long trips.

- Fuel pumps are a cause of motor home fires. The pump diaphragm may have a slight tear that isn't enough to keep the engine from running; gasoline forced through the tear leaks into the engine crankcase. If pressure causes the tear to rupture, the gasoline fumes in the crankcase might then cause an explosion. Prevent by frequent engine checks and good maintenance.

- The improper mounting of a generator can be a fire hazard if the exhaust from the generator overheats the motor home body. Also check the neoprene gasoline hoses on the tow vehicle or motor home; if the outer cover is brittle or shows any cracks, replace the hoses before they leak or rupture, causing a fire.

- Electrical fires are often the result of adding equipment. W.E. Von Pertz had an awning put on by a reputable dealer. A few hours later his motor home burned to the ground because a fastener used to secure the awning shorted out a hot wire. Stay alert for problems after any new work is done.

- Place fire extinguishers in convenient locations where they can be easily reached in an emergency. They must be large enough—or you must have enough of them to do an effective job on any fire. Chemical extinguishers lose their charge over a period of time, so have them checked annually.

- Turn off your propane valves at the bottles as soon as possible after detecting a fire.

- The accepted signal for help is to turn on your vehicle lights and blow the horn in series of three blasts, stop, three blasts. Repeat until help arrives.

- When parked with city water hookup, leave an extra hose attached to the faucet, ready to fight a fire. Use a "Y" connection if necessary.

Violent Summer Storms

Thunder and lightning storms are often accompanied by hail and followed by tornadoes. Hail can cause severe cosmetic damage to your RV, but you are in no danger as long as you stay inside your rig.

Lightning

Experts agree that the safest place to be during a lightning storm is inside your RV or tow vehicle. Lightning can cause damage to RV electrical appliances, such as radio, television, air conditioner, or refrigerator, *if* your AC power line is hooked up. Circuit breakers react too slowly to prevent damage from power surges generated by lightning if it strikes anywhere on the power line. To avoid this, unplug your AC power cord from the campground electrical receptacle during a severe lightning storm.

An alternative to unplugging the AC power is to buy an AC surge protector and install it between the RV power cord and electrical receptacle. There are several types with varying degrees of efficiency. The one we recommend for lightning protection costs $495 and is made by Lightning Elimination Association, 12516 Lakeland Road, Santa Fe Springs, CA 90670. Ask them for: P/N SE-(120) 20S.

If you are caught outside, stay away from flag poles, telephone poles, and tall trees. If you are fishing or playing golf, don't take your pole or clubs when you head for shelter. If you feel the hair on your head, arms, or neck starting to stand on end, throw yourself on the ground and lie as flat as possible.

Tornadoes

Tornadoes often follow violent thunderstorms and usually move from the southwest to the northeast. They occur most often between 3 and 7 p.m. and are more common in April, May, and June. No state is immune to tornadoes, but the areas most prone to them are the continental plains and along the Gulf Coast.

If you are on the highway and see a tornado traveling either with or toward you, chances are you'll outrun it if you can drive at *right angles* to it. Watch the sky and listen to the radio reports.

Tornado WATCH means that the counties indicated have conditions that can breed a tornado. There is no immediate danger except to remain alert.

Tornado WARNING means a tornado has been sighted or is moving toward the designated areas. Reports name the counties involved, so keep a map handy. County lines are usually defined with a thin blue line. Know which county you are driving in, and headed toward, so you'll know if you should seek shelter, change direction, or proceed forward.

If you are driving on the highway in a danger zone, look for shelter under a bridge or overpass. Get as far off the roadway as possible. The blinding rain that accompanies these storms obscures the view of passing motorists.

If you see a funnel-shaped cloud or hear a roar like that of an approaching train, leave the RV and crouch or lie against the most structurally protected area of the bridge. If you are in open country, experts recommend that you lie down in a ditch or ravine when you see or hear a tornado coming.

Caution! Tornadoes are accompanied by heavy rains, and in some areas that means flash floods can race through a ravine with tremendous speed and volume. It doesn't do much good to survive a tornado if you drown in the process.

If you are in a town, look for a sturdy building and go inside.

Stay away from windows and exterior doors.

Safety Tips From *Escapees* Magazines

- The commonly accepted distress signal is to blare your vehicle horn three times, stop a few seconds and repeat this procedure until help comes. Sometimes it is hard to know where the sound is coming from, so turn on your lights and flashing blinker signal so those coming to your aid can locate you.

- RVers must depend on each other in times of trouble. If you hear a distress signal, go immediately to see how you can help. Grab your fire extinguisher in case the problem is a fire.

- Whenever you are hooked up to city water, put a "Y" on the faucet and hook an extra hose to the side you are not connected to. We hope you'll never use the extra hose, but it could save your rig in the event of a fire when there is no time to disconnect a hose from the rig.

- A 12-volt boat horn will scare anyone prowling around your rig. Install the horn under or outside your rig with a control button inside. Push the button on and off several times, and the prowler will think he has set off an alarm. The cost is under $10, and the best time to buy is at the end of boating season when such items are on sale.

- If your RV has an aluminum frame window, place a bar in the channel (using a screw as a stop) to keep the window from being fully opened. It is easy to remove when you are at home and quick to install before you leave.

- Turn knobs on window awnings look the same whether locked or unlocked unless you look closely, so it is easy to take off without having them secured. Put a daub of red nail polish on the unlocked side, and you can tell at a glance if they are locked.

- Check the tow-vehicle hitch on a regular basis. That funny noise you think means a call for oil could be broken welds. Test your break-away switch too. When the cable is pulled, the trailer brakes are automatically applied.

- Never leave the window open beside the door when you are away from your RV. A burglar can cut the screen, reach inside and unlock the door.

Boondocking

Some RVers do not use free overnight parking, referred to as *boondocking,* because they don't know how to go about finding the "freebies;" others never boondock because they are afraid to do so.

On the other end of the pendulum, there are some who depend on free overnight parking because it is the only way they can afford to travel. But most of those who boondock do so simply because they have learned to use their self-contained RV.

Even when they stay in an RV park, some RVers never use the swimming pool or clubhouse. Because they don't need any amenities, they prefer to use the money they save on campground fees for other things. But probably the RVers who boondock the most do so because they don't like making reservations and being bound by time schedules.

Where do you find the freebies?

Most RVers prefer the free parking spaces along highways because they don't have to go out of their way to find them. The most commonly used are highway rest areas, truck stops and scenic viewpoints. The problem is that they are noisy, especially in summer when you have to leave windows open.

When traveling through towns where you need to buy a product such as tires, propane, or groceries, or when you need a service such as a Laundromat, beauty parlor, or restaurant, you can probably stay overnight in the parking lot where the product or service is sold if you ask the manager. Plan to arrive late in the day so that it will be near closing time when you are finished or so you'll have to wait overnight to have the service performed.

After making your purchase or arranging for next-day service, say that you are tired and don't want to drive any further. "Is there somewhere on your parking lot where we can stay overnight and not be in your way?"

When you purchased your RV, you paid a high price for self-containment. Use it whenever you can.

According to an Escapee Club survey, 78% of the surveyed members said they use overnight freebies at least occasionally and 63% said they use overnight freebies more than 25% of the time when traveling.

Finding the Freebies

Once you have experienced the freedom of choice that self-containment gives you, you will be ready to explore all the possibilities. There are thousands of little city and county parks across America where you can park from overnight to as long as 14 days absolutely free. And an impressive number of them even provide free water, free electricity, and a dump station. You can find out if a town has one by asking at the police station or at the chamber of commerce.

There are two important rules to remember when using freebies: Try to use the service or products of the person whose property you are parked on, and leave each place cleaner than you found it. For in-depth information on using freebies, read:

Survival of the RV Snowbirds, by Joe and Kay Peterson.

RoVing Publications
100 Rainbow Drive
Livingston, TX 77351
(800) 976-8377

When you first start using the freebies, you may feel more comfortable knowing it is a place that others use. If so, there are a couple of publications you may want to get:

• *Guide to Free Campgrounds,* by Don Wright, lists over 6000 *free* (or nearly free) campgrounds in the United States. Write:

Cottage Publications
420 S. 4th Street
Elkhart, Indiana.
(Phone:1-219-293-7553)

• *How To Travel America Coast to Coast And Stay Free Every Night* sells for $12.95 plus $3 shipping and handling. Write:

RV Guide
2420 N. Knoxville
Peoria, IL 61604-3645
(Phone: 1-800-475-0094)

Remember, circumstances change, so some of the places that were free at time of publication may no longer be free.

Locating Dump Stations

Some states are closing their roadside rest dump stations, but there are many other places where RVers who don't stay in commercial parks can find dump facilities (sometimes called sani-stations) to empty holding tanks.

- Check with tourist information centers. Usually someone knows where a dump station is located. Some even have a mimeographed list they will give you of dump stations within their state.

- State and national parks. Some are outside the pay gate. When the entrance booth is ahead of the facility, if you ask you may still be able to go in and dump free or for a minimal fee.

- City and town parks that allow overnight camping.

- Many Forest Service, Bureau of Land Management (BLM) and Corps of Engineer (COE) parks still have an "open gate" policy for *day use* which means you can use showers, fill with water, and dump without any charge.

- Military installations with a fam camp. (Usually limited to retired military people.)

- County fairgrounds (usually found on outskirts of the city). Some will allow you to use their dump station if you ask. Most have locked gates at night and on weekends.

- Sewage disposal plants: Gates open during working hours.

- Boat ramps frequently have a dump facility.

- RV service centers. Camping World stores allow free dumping, but others, like REC V (U-Haul), charge a fee.

- Gasoline stations. The 76 gas stations put out a directory showing which of their stations have dump facilities.

- Fraternal organizations, e.g. Elks, frequently have a parking area with a sani-dump, but it is generally for members only.

NOTE: Many RVers find it is easier to plan their travels to spend one or more nights a week in a campground or RV park. This allows them to dump, fill with water, and to catch up on cleaning and laundry while they take a break from travel.

Is Coyote Camping Legal?

Coyote camping is the term applied to long-term use of freebies that are found in desert or isolated areas. Most coyote camps are on government property. According to government literature, "The use of public lands by RV snowbirds has increased by 250% since 1978." Many are winter visitors from northern states. There have been as many as 20,000 vehicles parked on these public lands where there are no facilities.

The "public lands" are what is left of the historic public domain after private individuals, corporations, state and local governments, and federal agencies acquired the most desirable lands during the country's westward expansion in the last century. The remaining lands that nobody wanted come to 341 million acres that are scattered unevenly throughout the West. They are all that is left of America's "wide-open spaces."

The Bureau of Land Management (BLM) has control over 174 million acres in the lower western states and 167 million in Alaska. It must compromise between the increasingly competitive and conflicting demands of all Americans for use of that land.

For the past few years there has been a growing concern among RVers as to whether the federal government will someday put an end to the use of public lands by RVers. Some believe the inauguration of the new camping policy may be the first step in that direction. Others hope the new policy will provide a better way to handle sanitation, trash, and waste water while still permitting RV snowbirds to use public lands.

The BLM limits camping on public lands to 14 days in a single location. Those desiring to stay longer must either move their campsite a minimum of 25 miles or purchase a "seasonal permit." This allows them to remain up to eight months in designated camping areas that have been set aside for long-term camping in the California and southwestern Arizona deserts.

The long-use permit is only $25 a season. There is no discount for Golden Age and no prorating. You can obtain a permit from the BLM offices in California and Arizona.

Tips On Boondocking

- A Coleman lamp provides good light for most evening activities, and in a mini-motor home it throws off enough heat so you won't need to use a heater. Be sure to crack a vent or a window for proper ventilation.

- A catalytic heater uses less propane than the factory-installed furnace and doesn't run down batteries because there is no electric fan to circulate the air.

- Paint one-gallon plastic jugs with black paint. Fill with water and set them out in the sun. The black color absorbs the sun's heat. By night you have enough hot water to do dishes without using the water heater.

- Save the water pump from running the battery down by keeping water on hand in containers such as plastic milk jugs. Use the water jug instead of turning on the water when you want a drink, make coffee, etc.

- Conserve propane by keeping the water heater off except for once a day when you turn it on to heat water for bathing. Plan to shave and do dishes at this time also. The hot water heater is one of the most wasteful uses of propane if it is left on. At other times, heat small amounts of water in a teakettle on the stove top.

- If you plan to do a lot of boondocking, increase your self-containment by installing a catalytic heater which is more efficient than the propane furnace and does not require battery power to operate a fan.

- Invest in a macerator pump. With it, you can empty your gray and black water tanks through a garden hose into a house clean-out drain or a toilet.

- The best guidebook available for learning about overnight boondocking or long-term coyote camping is *Survival of the RV Snowbirds* by Joe and Kay Peterson.

(See books in address section.)

Tips On Traveling With Pets

- Give your pet a chance to get accustomed to travel by taking it on short trips. If your pet gets motion sickness, do not feed for at least four hours before starting a trip. Plan meals for night.

- Let dog exercise every few hours. (It helps the driver, too.) Throwing a ball or a Frisbee is a good exercise. Some places require dogs be kept on a leash, so be sure you take one with you.

- Always carry baggies with you when walking your dog in public places so you can pick up the droppings. Place your hand inside the bag, pick up the droppings, and as you remove your hand turn the bag inside out. Dispose of bag in a trash can.

- Do not allow pet to ride with its head out the window. Insects and dirt can become lodged in the eyes and cause serious problems.

- Don't leave pet alone in a parked car for more than a few moments. Temperatures inside a closed vehicle can rise very rapidly. If you leave your pet in the RV, be sure that windows are open enough to provide cross-ventilation. If you wouldn't be comfortable staying in the temperature, neither will your pet.

- Some campgrounds do not accept dogs and a few do not accept any type of pet. This includes some state parks, including those in Florida.

- Always keep your pet on a leash when you are in campgrounds. Make sure there is shade within range of the leash and that water is available. *Never* leave your dog leashed outside when you are away from the RV. Children may be tempted to tease the dog, causing an injury for which *you* may be held responsible. Dogs that are well behaved when their masters are present may whine or bark when they are left alone.

- Don't allow your dog to relieve itself on your neighbor's tires or anywhere in their defined camping space. All rules on traveling with a pet are based on consideration of your pet and other people. If you remember that, common sense will dictate proper behavior.

Protecting Pets from Mosquitoes

In our country, the mosquito is considered more of a nuisance than a threat since we don't have problems with malaria or yellow fever. But she is more than a pest. She is also a deadly enemy.

We say "she" because only the female bites. She lives twice as long as the male and she needs blood—lots of blood—to lay her quota of up to 300 eggs. Then she needs even more blood to develop the eggs. She gets this blood from both humans and animals.

So we spray ourselves with repellents when we are going into infested areas. But too often we neglect to protect our dog—and it is the dog who is in grave danger. People who have previously lived in a city, or an area where mosquitoes aren't prevalent, don't realize the danger that lurks in highly infested areas such as Alaska, Canada, or the southeastern states.

Your dog can easily contract heart worm from a single mosquito bite! The good news is that you can prevent heart worm by just giving your dog an inexpensive pill every day. If you skip more than an occasional day, and your dog has been any place where there are mosquitoes, you are endangering his life if you resume the medicine without first having him tested for heart worms. If a dog already has heart worms, the preventative medicine will kill him. Check with a veterinarian on the need for testing and the proper dosage since the animal's weight determines the dosage.

The bad news is that many of our pets won't willingly take the tablet. You end up trying to trick the dog into taking it by disguising it in food or, you hold the dog and force the pill down its throat—or you decide it is too much hassle and stop trying.

Now a better solution comes packaged as a new, concentrated medicine called Heartgard (Ivermectin) tablets that you only have to give once a *month* instead of once a *day*. These new preventative tablets are expensive—six tablets cost around $10. But six tablets is a six-months supply. Some feel the convenience and elimination of a daily fight is worth the extra cost.

Driving or Towing an RV

A 1972 study by the National Transportation Safety Board (NTSB) indicated that driver error is a principal factor in RV accidents. This is because many drivers don't appreciate the difference between RV driving and normal automobile or pickup truck driving. Errors in judgment include both the lack of knowledge of what to do in unexpected situations and taking unnecessary risks.

For your safety, as well as that of others on the highway, you need to reevaluate your driving skills. This begins with an understanding and an awareness of the problems.

Awareness

- When an accident occurs with a motor home, injuries are greater if any passengers are standing up or walking around. When the motor home hits—or is hit by—another object, the sudden impact can cause passengers to fly through the air with the force of a missile.

- Motor homes and pickups towing trailers lose power hill-climbing and they can "run away" in steep downgrades.

- Vehicle stability is affected by overloading the vehicle, by sucking air currents of passing trucks, and by strong crosswinds.

- There can be a sudden failure of brakes, drive trans, or steering units.

- Tires blow more easily because of the vehicle's weight.

- RVs cannot stop as quickly as passenger cars, so you must anticipate road conditions well ahead. Even minor changes in road grade or pavement quality can cause loss of control.

- RVs require more room to turn, are more difficult to back up, and need more side-to-side clearance.

Learning to drive again

Taking all of the above into consideration, you not only need to have a full understanding of the differences between handling an RV and driving a passenger car, but you also need to learn how to *adapt* your previous driving skills to accommodate the differences.

Practice

Before you take off on strange highways, get the feel of your RV just as you did when you first learned to drive. Find a vacant parking lot and lay out an imaginary driveway and streets by using string borders or placing a board on tin cans. Practice backing up and parking until you can perform these skills without disturbing the string or board boundaries. Only then will you fully appreciate your RV's width, length, and turning radius.

The next training step is to learn what the transmission can do. Find a highway with minimum traffic and hills and valleys. Do your practice in early morning hours when traffic is lightest. Learn how to use the transmission to make acceleration easiest on the engine and deceleration easiest on the brakes. Remember the different turning radius and slow down for curves. Keep an eye out for signs and other side-of-the-road obstructions.

Cruising skills

Now you are ready for the real test—a highway drive that takes you over new turf. Remember to start off slowly in first gear (your engine is pulling a lot of weight from a dead stop) and wait for adequate clearance before you pull into the traffic.

After you've reached your cruising speed and feel in control of the situation, you still need to stay alert to the suction movement sometimes caused by passing trucks. If this is a problem with your rig, drive on the far side of your lane to put as much room as possible between you and passing trucks.

If you are towing a trailer and you start to feel sway (fishtailing), tap the trailer hand brake. *Don't step on your tow-vehicle foot brake as it will increase the swaying.* Apply your trailer hand brake while your foot presses the gas pedal.

Passing

When you pass a vehicle in front of you, remember that it takes more room, and more time, than passing with an automobile. Signal your intention and move slowly from one lane to the other. It is safe to pull back into the lane when the passed vehicle is fully visible in your passenger side view mirror. Signal!

When a truck or another RV passes *you,* flash your lights to signal when it is safe for the passing vehicle to pull back in front of you. Most truckers appreciate this simple courtesy. Watch for the same signal from courteous drivers that you pass.

If your speed goes under 45 when you are passing, downshift manually into second gear until you complete the passing. Using second gear gives you better control and quicker response at this lower speed.

If you find yourself stuck in the passing lane, don't panic or try to overtake high speed vehicles in the slower lane. When you have proper clearance, turn your signal on and return to the cruising lane.

Driving on steep grades

Motor homes as well as trailers in tow can "run away" on steep down grades. Proper braking is essential. *Do NOT* hold your foot on the brake peddle, however tempting it may be. Overheated brakes are useless!

When you see the downgrade sign warning truckers to shift into lower gear, do likewise. Moderate downgrades can often be handled completely by downshifting, but on long, steep grades, stay in second gear (or go down into first if necessary) until your speed increases to the point where you feel a need to brake. Apply the brakes *hard* for a few seconds and *then get off the pedal.*

If you are towing a trailer, you can also apply the trailer hand brake to slow down.

When you are climbing hills, you can feel the engine's load. The higher you climb above sea level, the less power your vehicle will have because the air gets increasingly thinner. Downshift even before it seems necessary and it will ease the strain on your engine.

Downshifting gives higher engine torque (pulling power).

When climbing hills, never hold your accelerator all the way to the floor as this can cause the engine to overheat. (It also wastes fuel.) Keep downshifting and allow your speed to drop as long as you can keep moving. Upshift to second gear when your speed increases to about 35 miles per hour.

Hazardous Driving Conditions

Whenever possible, get off the road if driving is hazardous. Sit in a roadside rest or a parking lot, overnight if necessary, when there is heavy fog, high winds, or blinding rain. If you're caught on the highway, get well off the pavement.

If you must drive on icy roads, drive slowly using your lowest gear to reduce vehicle speed. Remember, bridges are often icy even when the rest of the road is not. Watch out for *"black ice"*—that thin layer of ice you can't see. Braking on ice can cause you to skid sideways or turn over. Pump the brakes instead of pushing the pedal down.

On uneven roads with potholes, keep moving slowly. If you hit a pothole with rigidly applied brakes all the road shock is transferred to the vehicle suspension and springs.

Tips on driving or towing an RV

- RV noises can dull the sound of emergency vehicle sirens. Keep checking your rearview mirrors.

- Avoid night driving when visibility is limited.

- Plan your routes to avoid freeway rush hours. If you find yourself caught in a traffic jam, take the next exit and find a place to park until the traffic dies down.

- Beware of pulling off onto questionable terrain that might not support the weight of your heavy vehicle.

- If you make an emergency stop, pull off the road as far as possible, turn on your flashers, and set warning flares or reflectors. Use a CB radio to summon help.

- Don't go down unfamiliar, unmapped roads. Check them out first if there is a question that you may not be able to turn around or back out.

- When you stop for gasoline, make it a practice to check all your systems, including the tires, and the hitch and safety chains on towed vehicle. Check your own oil and transmission fluid. Some attendants will purposely not push the dip stick all the way in so they can sell you extra oil.

Unleaded Gasoline

According to tests reported in 1987, the minute amount of lead allowed by EPA in gasoline (and it's going down to zero) can cause damage to valve seats.

In 1987 Chrysler Corporation issued a "customer advisory" stating that "Valve seat wear is aggravated by operating at high speeds and loads, particularly for long periods of time."

Engines that were designed to use *unleaded* gasoline were made with hardened valve seats to compensate for the removal of lead. Older vehicles and those with engines designed for *leaded* gasoline don't have that protection. The lead in gasoline creates a cushion between valve and valve seats that minimizes wear.

RV experts have been warning us since 1984 that taking the lead out of gasoline is damaging to leaded gas engines—especially under severe use, such as the demand put on RV tow vehicles and motor home engines.

While more of the states are pushing their maximum mileage back up to 65 m.p.h. on interstate freeways, the manufacturers are warning us of the damage to engines caused by increased speeds! Our natural tendency is to drive as fast as the law allows. Or faster—when you think you can get away with it.

In addition to the engine stress caused by higher speeds, an engine must work harder when it is pulling the heavy load of RV trailers and motor homes. If there are long, continuous hours of running, it will even further aggravate the situation. When you add all three—overloading, continuous operation, and higher speeds—you are, in effect, doubling the mileage being put on the engine.

One answer is to have the cylinder heads rebuilt with hardened valve-seat inserts. Another alternative is to buy lead additives such as Bardahl or Powershield by the Lubrizol Corporation. Powershield was used in one of the tests which proved that lead-replacement additives do offer protection to valve seats.

The best answer is to lighten your load and *SLOW DOWN.*

How To Increase Gas Mileage

Most experts agree that you can save more fuel by changing your driving habits than you can by purchasing and installing the many so-called fuel-saving devices that are on the market. Here are some tips to help you save money by increasing your mileage.

- **Avoid sudden stops.** If you are alert to what is happening around and ahead of you, there will be no need for sudden braking. By watching ahead, you know when you have to change lanes or ease to a stop. Each time you apply the brakes, you are losing energy from your engine. Instead of jamming on the brakes, take your foot off the gas and allow the weight of your vehicle and the drag of the engine to slowly ease you to a stop. This will also give your brake system a longer life.

- **Avoid jackrabbit starts.** Slowly press the gas pedal down until you've gained momentum. Sudden starts use up extra fuel.

- **Use a cruise control** when driving on level terrain. When driving in hill country, turn off the cruise control and use your judgment as to when to accelerate and decelerate on hills.

- **Use a vacuum gauge.** If you are a poor judge of when you are straining your motor, install a vacuum gauge and drive according to its dictates, especially when climbing hills.

- **Shifting gears.** Don't use the lower, less efficient passing gear if you have an automatic transmission. Ease off on the accelerator as you feel the gears shifting.

- **Check tires and wheels.** For best mileage, tires should be fully inflated to the manufacturer's recommended air pressure, but don't exceed the amount stamped on the sidewall of the tire. Towing on under inflated tires can lessen your mileage and can cause the tires to wear out more quickly.

- **Tires should have equal pressure.** If you drive with tires that have unequal pressure, it hurts your gas mileage even more than having all tires under inflated. When you run on one under inflated tire on the front of your vehicle, it can cause "drag" that forces the engine to work harder and thus use more gas.

How To Increase Gas Mileage

- **Proper wheel alignment** is very important. If you have ever pushed a shopping cart with a cocked wheel, you can imagine the extra energy that is required when your engine is trying to push your vehicle if a wheel is out of alignment.

- **Warming the engine** is an old-fashioned idea and a waste of fuel. When you turn on the key, wait a few seconds to allow the fluids to circulate and the oil to get around the bearings, then drive slowly away. In cold weather, your automatic choke will order the carburetor to pump in an extra-rich mixture and the engine will warm better with slow, easy driving than by allowing it to idle while you sit in the driveway.

- **Don't idle your motor** for any stop that is longer than one minute. If you are stopped by train crossings or highway traffic controllers, turn off the key. Restarting a warm engine costs almost nothing in fuel energy.

- **Tune-ups** can give you as much as a 10 percent increase in mileage. A well-tuned engine starts quicker and runs more efficiently. A tune-up should include checking spark plugs and changing your air filter.

- **Use two air filters** instead of just one to increase the air flow. A sequential method advocated by many RVers is to throw the bottom filter away, put the top filter on the bottom, and then add a new one on top.

- **Slow down.** If you drive at 50 m.p.h. instead of 70, you will save up to 20 per cent on your gas bill, not to mention how much you can save on speeding tickets!

Hints On Reading Maps

Every map has a north indicator, but that is little help unless you know which direction you are facing. A compass mounted to the dash is an excellent tool. Another important tool is a hi-liter (transparent) marking pen so you can mark route numbers, road side rests, or anything of interest that will make the trip interesting.

You also need a small light for map reading at night and a magnifying glass. The final item is a good collection of road maps—both state and major cities. (The ones put out by the American Automobile Association are best, but are for AAA members only.)

Our interstate highway numbering system is set up so that (for one- and two-digit numbers) even numbers run east and west and odd numbers run north and south.

Study the legend as it i tells you, among other things, the types of roads and the symbol for rest areas. Maps often use different legends.

As you plan your route, study the options you have of alternate routes between your present location and your destination. That way you can put some variety into your travels instead of always taking the major interstate roads.

Once you have agreed on a route, the navigator can follow the map and have a good idea of what is coming up. Rest stops are marked on most maps with a distinctive symbol, and there are mileage indicators between stars, pointers, or towns that enable you to determine exactly where you are on the map.

When nearing cities, know in advance what route you are following or need to change to. Look to see if there are other routes in conjunction with yours that may confuse the driver. Sometimes the road you want is identified by another reference, so be aware of all other names and route numbers ahead of time.

The navigator should be checking carefully as you approach or leave any towns or route changes. Try to advise the driver of a turn or exit early enough to give sufficient time to get into the correct lane.

Driving Tips

- Check tire inflation in the morning before you start traveling. (Tires need to be cool.) Some radial tires look as if they have a low pressure even when they are at the proper inflation. Use a reliable tire gauge and put in the correct amount of air.

- To keep the spare tire cover from rotting out on the bottom due to an accumulation of water, cut a tiny hole in the bottom of the cover so the water can escape.

- If you have scratches on the outside of your RV, cover them before rust forms. Touch-up paint is available in every color. To get a perfect match, buy it from the RV manufacturer.

- Watch out for locked brakes, especially on trailers. When brakes lock up they will cause bearings to overheat and burn out due to the transfer of heat to the bearings. When you apply brakes and feel a drag afterwards, the brakes have probably failed to release. By backing up a few feet, you can usually cause brakes to release. If you suspect that your brakes did fail to release, stop in a few miles and check the drum for overheating. If it's too hot to touch, it means the brakes are still being applied on that wheel. If this is not corrected, you can be sure your wheel bearings will be burned out in 50-or-so miles of driving. Normally the cause for this is that your brake adjustment is off.

- Attach a wide-angle mirror to the bottom of your side view mirrors for better visibility of vehicles that are running along side you on the passenger side. A wide-angle lens in the back window of a motor home allows you to see small autos that hug your rear bumper.

- You can avoid carrying a lug wrench if you have a half-inch drive socket set in your tool box. A standard half-inch socket set will fit every lug in your RV with the possible exception of a Class-A motor home.

- If your running lights flicker on and off, gently rub a piece of fine sandpaper over the contact points to clean off any rust. Then spray them lightly with WD-40, or coat them with a little vaseline.

- A rubber band around the toilet tissue and paper towels will keep them from unrolling during travel.

Driving Tips

- If you tow a standard trailer, buy a ball hitch and mount it on the *front* bumper of your tow vehicle. When you have to back into a tight spot, block the trailer and unhitch it. Then turn the tow vehicle around and attach trailer to the front bumper. Now you can see where the RV is going, and you will also have better maneuverability.

- To get out of a tight space when the angle is wrong, disconnect the trailer (be sure to block it!) and move the tow vehicle so you can back from a better angle. Now attach the trailer to the front or back hitch ball and you can get out.

Emergency Equipment Suggestions

If you cannot fix the problem yourself, you will still need to have the necessary items for an emergency repair if someone stops to help you. The following are the bare essentials. You many also want to add your own special items to this list.

- Good quality jumper cables.
- Jack and lug wrench for changing tires.
- Spare radiator hose—type you can bend into any shape.
- Extra fan belts.
- Extra oil and extra transmission fluid.
- Extra light bulbs for tail lights, signal lights, brake lights, and running lights.
- Extra fuses.
- Small hand tools.
- Roll of electrical tape and bailing wire.

We highly recommend that you subscribe to one of the emergency road service providers who will assist you in tire changes and small repairs and will tow your RV or tow rig to a garage if that is necessary.

Cleaning RV Bathroom

- Porcelain sinks: You can make a stain remover by mixing:

    1 Tbs lemon juice with

    3 Tbs of either borax or cream of tartar

    4 Tbs hydrogen peroxide

- After you clean the toilet bowl, spray sides with Pam or with a spray wax such as Pledge. It will make cleanups easier.

- An old toothbrush works well for cleaning the groove around the top of RV toilets.

- Cotton swabs wet with liquid detergent can get into the tiny dirt-collecting areas at toilet cover hinge.

Tub and Shower

- Polish the sides and bottom of the shower with a wax polish every three months to reduce mineral deposits and make cleanup easier. Any good car wax will work.

- Fiberglass tubs, showers, and sinks are hard to keep clean and some commercial cleaners ruin the finish. Laundry stain removers (e.g. Shout and Clorox PreWash) work beautifully. The ones in spray bottles are easier to use.

- Another way is to sprinkle baking soda on a damp sponge and scrub shower. Dry with a clean cloth.

- Tub/shower drain. Put a pompon of coarse nylon net in the shower drain to collect hair and scum. When it needs cleaning, take it outside and rinse at the water hookup.

- When the shower head gets clogged from lime and mineral deposits, remove and soak it in vinegar.

- Rub bathroom fixtures with a cloth dampened in kerosene to remove the scum. If you have chrome fixtures, try wetting them with cold water, then rubbing with a newspaper.

- To eliminate or prevent mildew on a plastic shower curtain, place it in the washing machine with several bath towels. Add a half cup of detergent and a half cup of baking soda. In the rinse cycle, add a cup of vinegar and a few drops of mineral oil and it will remain pliable. Cut the hem off as it collects water and becomes a breeding place for mildew.

Cleaning RV Kitchen

- For severe refrigerator odors, try charcoal briquettes or an open dish of vanilla on a shelf. Empty the vanilla before you travel!

- If sink drain becomes clogged with grease, pour a cup of baking soda in the drain. Follow with a kettle of boiling water.

- If your RV sink is stainless steel, you can remove streaks by rubbing them with olive oil. A cloth dampened with alcohol will remove water spots. If rust appears, rub that area with lighter fluid. After rust disappears, wipe with your kitchen cleaner.

- Use coarse nylon net for dish rags. It can be used many times before discarding and it won't scratch Teflon.

- Cleaning thermos: Add a tablespoon of soda to a partly filled thermos jug and soak for a half hour. Wash and dry.

- Use baking soda and a damp sponge to clean the cutting board.

- You can clean the blades and cutter on an electric can opener by running a paper towel through the cutter.

- If you line the area under the burners with aluminum foil, the next cleanup will be easier.

- Place a dish of undiluted white distilled vinegar in the center of the oven and let it sit overnight. In the morning, rinse the oven with warm water.

- Clean stove top with ammonia and water to make it shine.

- Place a bath towel in the bottom of tub or shower and put oven racks, burner grates, knobs and stove tray on it. Add enough water to cover and one-fourth to one-half cup of dish washer granules to the water. Soak for an hour, rinse, and dry.

- Vegetable cooking odors will disappear if you place an open dish of vinegar by the stove when you cook.

- Burned on foods? Moisten pan with water. Sprinkle baking soda on burned spots. Rub with a damp sponge and then rinse.

- To remove brown grease spots on the bottom of an electric frying pan, place the pan in a large plastic bag containing a cloth saturated with ammonia. Close bag with a rubber band. (Leave handle containing electric element outside the bag.) In a few hours, remove pan and you can wash spots off with ease.

Cleaning RV

- Use a damp sheet of fabric softener to clean mini blinds. It eliminates the static that collects dust. Or use a soft cloth dampened with alcohol. In either case, if you wrap it around a rubber spatula, it will easily reach into the tiny slats.
- Bunch nylon net into a pompon to clean the dust off window and door screens.
- To cover scratches on furniture or cabinet doors, rub a brown crayon on it and then buff well with a soft, dry cloth. The wax from the crayon fills in the scratch.
- Old toothbrushes are great for cleaning combs and silverware. It is also good for cleaning the ridges around RV windows where the screen fits. Use cotton swabs for areas that the toothbrush cannot reach.
- If the RV heater won't light, the pilot may be clogged with dust. Try blowing out the dust with a bendable plastic milk straw.
- To restore luster to aluminum chairs, use a stiff brush dipped in household detergent to remove the rust and dirt. Go over the chair with a steel wool soap pad, rinse, and then dry with a clean cloth. To lengthen the time between cleaning, polish it with car wax or a product such as Protect All.
- Clean your razor by soaking it in a glass of vinegar.
- Vinegar removes mineral deposits as well as coffee and tea stains from ceramic or glass cups and pots.
- Remove price decals by painting them with several coats of vinegar. Let it set a few minutes, and the decal will wash off.
- Washing socks? If you add a quarter-cup of vinegar to the last rinse, it will remove soap and lint and make them softer.
- A strong solution of bleach and soapy water will remove most mildew and deter new growth. If mildew causes stains, try rubbing problem spots with lemon juice or vinegar.
- Sprinkle baking soda on your carpet. Let it stand 30 minutes, then vacuum up. It helps to eliminate odors.

Fighting Bug Invasions

- In summer, bugs can be a real problem on both the inside and outside. Some of them stick like glue to windshields and the front of your vehicle. The "love bugs," which swarm from Florida to central Texas every spring and fall, leave an acid residue that damages paint. They must literally be scrubbed off. To avoid scratching the paint or windshield, try using a piece of carpet remnant as a scrubber that won't scratch.

- To avoid damage when you are driving through infested areas, keep your vehicle waxed and bugs will be easier to wash off.

- Apply wax to chrome bumpers, too.

- Radiators collect bugs too. When you stop, use a wire brush to clean the bugs off the coils. If you notice your motor is running hot, stop and brush off the bugs. It could be that they are blocking the necessary air flow.

- To avoid attracting bugs inside the RV, try using yellow bulbs outside your RV. Spray a flying insect product on and around all window and door edges. Or purchase *Screen Pruf* at a hardware store (not available in all states). Brush it on your screen door and it will keep the bugs off for a long time.

- If you are invaded by ants, sprinkle salt along the baseboard and in the corners.

- For roaches, sprinkle borax along the back and corners of cupboard shelves. Borax is poisonous, so take precautions around pets and children.

- The ear tab (found in farm supply store) used on cattle can be pinned on a screen door to keep flies away.

- Whenever you close up your RV for a few months or put it in storage, hang a pest strip inside the compartments in back of your reefer, water tank, and furnace.

- Place moth balls in your closets and also in your pantry as they will discourage more than just moths.

Uses For Baking Soda

Baking soda cleans without scratching, absorbs odors, neutralizes acids, and smothers flames.

- Mix three tablespoons of baking soda in one quart warm water to clean the following items.

    (1) Comb and brush: Swish in solution. Rinse and dry.

    (2) Fishing rod and line. Sponge to remove odors.

    (3) Clean the glass door on your oven.

    (4) Refrigerator: Clean refrigerator inside and out.

    (5) Silverware: Soak 30 minutes and it will sparkle.

    (6) Windshield: Clean inside and out. Rinse and dry with soft cloth or paper towel.

    (7) Tired feet: soak in above solution.

- To clean vinyl or plastic seat covers and dashboard, sprinkle baking soda on damp sponge and rub clean. Wipe off with clean moist sponge.

- Golf irons: Sprinkle soda on damp sponge and scour.

- Hands and fingernails: Rub dry soda on moistened hands. It will remove pine pitch and grease.

- Car ash tray. Cover bottom of ash tray with soda about an eighth of an inch thick. Use it to snuff out butts.

- Closets: Store an open box in your closets. Set it inside a plastic container and wedge between other items so it won't spill. If it does spill, vacuum it up.

- Mouthwash: Use one teaspoon in half glass water.

- Shoes: Sprinkle some in your shoes to cut foot odor.

- Use it for toothpaste, on real teeth or dentures

- Burns (minor) or poison ivy: Use enough soda and water to make a paste and apply gently to affected area.

- Bath: use a cup soda in tub of water for muscle relaxer, itching skin, or sunburn.

Uses for Baking Soda

- Self-contained with limited water supply? Take a sponge bath of soda and water.
- Sprinkle soda over stored fish hooks to prevent rust.
- Battery corrosion. Add one tablespoon soda to one quart water and paint terminals with a brush dipped in that solution. Rinse, dry, and coat with Vaseline.
- Did your pet get too close to a porcupine? Make a solution of two teaspoons of soda to one cup of vinegar. Pat on the quills. Wait ten minutes. Reapply. Wait another ten minutes and then pull out quills.
- Baking soda is excellent for smothering fires—especially grease fires. Always keep an open box handy near the stove.
- To prevent spillage, pour the soda into an empty coffee can or similar container with a lid.
- Engine fire: Turn off ignition. Toss soda from windward side of engine if fire extinguisher runs out.

Uses for a hair dryer

Full-time RVers find ways to make the items they carry do double duty. Here are some other uses for your hair dryer.

- On cold days, use it to dry your dog's hair, too.
- Makes a quick job of defrosting refrigerator.
- Blow steam off the bathroom mirror.
- Blow bugs out the window or off the dashboard.
- Cold feet? Warm them up with a hair dryer!
- On chilly nights, use it to preheat the sheets.
- Also great for thawing frozen hoses and water lines if you didn't go south soon enough.
- When sealing a leak or crack with silicone, use a hair dryer on high heat to make silicone flow into the crack like solder. Don't hold hair dryer too close or it will blow silicone out of the crack.
- Remove an unwanted decal from RV skin by blowing heat from hair dryer on it. Then it should peel right off.

Care Of Clothing

- When you hand-wash sweaters, try a capful of cream hair rinse in the final rinse water.
- For longer-wearing pantyhose, add just a little starch to the rinse water. Starch makes them more resistant to runs and easier to put on.
- Your nylons will last longer if you place them in an ice cube tray, fill tray with water, and then freeze. When the water is frozen solid, place tray on refrigerator shelf to thaw gradually. Remove nylons and dry them.
- If you end up with several good nylons that don't match, place them in a glass or enamel pan and boil for three minutes. They'll all come out the same shade.
- Spray white tennis shoes heavily with starch and they will stay clean longer.
- If you scorch a white shirt while ironing, take a piece of stale bread, moisten it and rub over scorched area.
- If your iron gets sticky, try running it back and forth over a paper sack sprinkled with salt.
- Buttons will stay on blouses and shirts longer if you put a drop of clear fingernail polish on the threads.
- To remove ring-around-the-collar stain from a shirt or a blouse, try this: Pour ammonia into a saucer, then dip a wet fingernail-type (soft bristle) brush in the ammonia and rub it over the stain before placing the garment in the washing machine.
- To remove grease spots, rub them lightly with a mixture of table salt dissolved in ammonia.
- Wrap a rubber band around each end of a coat hanger and your garments will be less likely to slip off.
- Hangers will stay on the rods during travel if you turn the hangers with open side towards door or crimp the hanger loop.
- Sewing emblem patches on clothing? Put a few dabs of white glue on the back of the emblem and then press it in position. Let it set a few minutes before you stitch by hand or machine and it won't turn out lopsided.

Cooking Tips

- To keep onions from sprouting and becoming soft, wrap each one in aluminum foil.
- To keep potatoes from sprouting, store them with apples.
- Store whole lemons in a tightly sealed jar of water and keep in refrigerator. They will yield more juice.
- If potato chips or crackers get stale, put them under the broiler for a few seconds only and they will become crisp again. Be careful! They brown easily.
- You can perk up wilting lettuce by soaking it for an hour in cold water to which you have added a little lemon juice.
- Clam shells open themselves if you put them in the freezer for ten minutes before you want to use them.
- Salt will flow freely even in humid weather if you keep a few grains of rice in the shaker.
- Popcorn will pop bigger if you store the kernels in the freezer until ready to use.
- To get rid of the fat in soup or stew, drop a few ice cubes into the pot. Stir, and the fat will cling to the cubes. Be sure to remove cubes before they melt.
- If muffins stick to tin pan, place pan on a wet towel. They'll slide right out.
- If butter is too hard to spread, soften it by inverting a heated pan over the butter dish for a few minutes.
- Catsup will flow easily if you first insert a drinking straw as far as possible into the bottle.
- To find out if an egg is fresh without breaking the shell, immerse it in a pan of cool, salted water. A fresh one sinks to the bottom. Bad eggs will float.
- Pancakes won't stick or smoke if you first rub the griddle with salt instead of butter or oil.
- Bacon won't curl while frying if you dip it in cold water and then dry it on a paper towel before cooking.
- You can soften lumpy sugar by placing a slice of fresh bread in the package.

Cooking Tips

- Spread butter or margarine on the cut edge of cheese to keep it from drying out.

- For quick baked potatoes, boil the potatoes in their skins for ten minutes. Then pop them into a very hot oven.

- Poke a hole in the center of hamburger after shaping. The center will cook quickly and when the hamburgers are done, holes will be gone.

- Before you go to bed, place a package of rolls in the gas oven with just the pilot turned on. They will be ready to eat and will taste freshly baked in the morning.

- Egg whites will whip more quickly if you place the eggs in cold water for a while before breaking them.

- You can cut whipping time in half and have firmer whipped cream by adding a few drops of lemon juice to cream.

- For dessert, pour ginger ale on top of watermelon cubes.

- Wrap green grapes in waxed paper and then store in the freezer for a delicious snack.

- Another snack: Place sardines on buttered toast, sprinkle with grated cheese, and broil a few minutes.

- Spread tortilla chips on a cookie sheet. Cover with a thin layer of grated cheese and broil till cheese melts.

- Sprinkle a little ground nutmeg on apple cider to give it a zingy flavor.

- Dust a little flour in the skillet before you fry eggs. Keeps the grease from spattering over stove top.

- You will cut cooking time in half if you bake meat loaf in muffin tins instead of a loaf pan. Easier to serve, too.

- If you grease the rim of the cooking pot with margarine or cooking oil, vegetables won't boil over.

- Wrap garlic bread in foil, but leave top open partway if you want the bread crusty instead of soggy.

- A good substitution for nuts in a recipe is to use the same amount of rice cereal.

Cooking Tips

- No need to carry a meat tenderizing hammer in your rig. Just put your regular hammer to a dual purpose. Wash well and pound away.

- Cover link sausage with water in a pan. Just barely bring to a boil and drain. Then put the pan in the sink and run cold water over the sausages. When cold, let them dry. Refrigerate or freeze. There will be no splattering of grease when you heat the sausages.

- You'll have a dry picnic basket or cooler if you freeze water in plastic jugs. Water can be used after ice melts.

- Making soup? Cut vegetables and onion first. Cut celery last. Celery will take the onion smell off your hands.

- When sour milk is called for in a recipe and you don't have any, add one tablespoon vinegar to one cup of fresh milk.

- For a lower calorie frosting, use one package instant pudding containing Nutrasweet, one cup skim milk, and eight ounces lite Cool Whip.

- To keep a hamburger patty from shrinking, press your finger into the middle of the patty to make a deep indentation, but not all the way through.

- Store potatoes in a cool, dark place, ideally about 50 degrees F. Refrigeration will convert potato starch to sugar, and warm temperatures will cause potatoes to shrivel and dry out.

- Low-fat yogurt is a good substitute for mayonnaise and cream in salad dressing recipes. Great on baked potatoes, too.

- To make bread crumbs without a mess, place dried-out bread in a sealed plastic bag and then roll over it with rolling pin.

- Butter leftover bread slices, season with garlic salt, toast, and cut into cubes for croutons used in soup and salads.

- Cookies stale? Don't throw them away! Grate them in a food processor or blender and store in a freezer container. Use in recipes that call for graham cracker crumbs.

Making Storage Holders

- Cardboard cores from paper towels and toilet paper are excellent for storing electrical cords. Cover them with attractive contact paper for durability.

- Plastic dishpans and colorful kitchen storage bins are ideal to use on closet shelves to separate various items and will allow better usage of space.

- Plastic see-through shoe boxes make ideal storage boxes for closet shelves so you can see at a glance what each one contains.

- You can organize your things better if you partition deep cabinets with Masonite. Separate the space into two shelves or into definite compartments.

- On bedroom wall, mount adjustable shelves (sold in discount and building supply stores) for storage of books or other items. To make sure they will hold up to travel on rough roads, screw the bracing rods into the wall in several places even if you have to drill new holes. Add a molding trim to the exposed shelf edges to hold items in place as you travel.

- Fasten colorful shoe bags to walls either inside or outside closets for storage of belts, scarves, or small craft and hobby items. Buy a large bag and cut it in half so you can use one part in the bedroom and the other in the bathroom for toilet articles.

- A shoe bag also works behind the back seat of your tow vehicle for storage of maps, magnifying glass, and similar travel items.

- Square half-gallon milk cartons make good shoe storage boxes. Wash and dry, then cover with contact paper. They stack well in single, double, or triple units. Good for tool and gadget storage.

- If you have a camper or mini with a cab-over bed that you don't use, put the space to good use by converting it into cabinets. Attach sliding doors to the front.

- A shoe box makes a good place to store lids from storage bowls and pans so they won't scatter during travel.

- Place a small curtain rod, the spring-tension kind, in front of the refrigerator shelf to keep items from falling out.

- Ask at your supermarket for a couple of boxes that wine comes in. It makes a perfect place to store shoes neatly in the closet.

Miscellaneous Tips

- When leaving your RV, leave the closet doors open occasionally to air out the clothing. Unwrap and store extra bars of soap on your closet shelf. Gives nice odor.

- Want to keep your shoes clean when you are parked in a muddy campground? Slip a plastic sack around your shoe and hold it in place with a rubber band around your leg.

- If the carpet does get muddy, sprinkle cornstarch on damp mud spots. Let it set for about 15 minutes and then vacuum.

- Postage stamps stick together in humid climates. Put them in the freezer for a few minutes and you can pull them apart.

- If you don't have one of the new automatic switch-over refrigerators and you run it on electric, plug in a night light and you can tell at a glance if the power is disconnected.

- Tuck a sheet of laundry softener in your soiled laundry to counter odors. You can still use the softener in the dryer as the damp clothes will rejuvenate it.

- Rub dishwater detergent on the outside of the skillet before cooking over a campfire. The soot will wash right off.

- If you spend time in the desert areas, your plants need frequent attention. Fill a glass baking dish or similar container with an inch-layer of colorful aquarium rock. Place small plant pots on the rock. Add water to just below the surface of the rock. Gives them the humidity they need.

- If you store your RV in a dry desert climate be sure to fill sinks and tub with water before you leave. The water will evaporate putting some moisture into the air and will prevent wood from drying and cracking. Fill the toilet bowl also to keep the toilet seal from around the valve from drying out.

- To keep your outdoor carpet from blowing away, pound a 20-penny nail and fender washer in each corner at the edge. This eliminates any worry of tripping over rocks.

- To secure a throw rug inside the RV, use double-sided tape along the edges, or even just at the corners and it won't slip on linoleum. If rug is on carpet, use short macrame pins on each corner to hold it in place.

Miscellaneous Tips

- To secure hose into the sewer outlet, use a three-inch "rubber donut." It wedges in for a tighter fitting, thus sealing it against sewer gases. It will slip on easier if you cut one side.

- Propane bottles sometimes "pop off" in hot weather due to pressure buildup. To prevent this, when you mount a newly-filled bottle, "top it off" by switching to that tank for a day.

- If you need to replace LP gas tanks, valves, etc., go to an LP gas company—not an RV store. They sell the same products as RV stores but at a much cheaper price.

- After you clean the aluminum frame around RV windows, coat the aluminum with a clear acrylic to cut down problems with black stain.

- Has your diamond ring lost its sparkle? Oil on your hands and wash water that comes in contact with the diamond leaves a film on it that dulls the refracting property. To bring back the luster, wash it in household ammonia. It should be a fresh bottle —not one that has been under the sink for months. For the best results, rinse your diamond daily in ammonia.

- "Wet and Wipe" travel pads are good for removing stains on clothing. Immediately after spillage, place a paper towel under the fabric and rub upper surface with the wipe. The stain will come off on the paper towel.

- Stubborn stains inside glass vases will come off if you dampen the interior and then add a little toilet bowl cleaner. Let it stand for ten minutes and then wash the stains or film away.

- Storing a partially-used steel wool soap pad in the same box with unused ones will keep it from rusting.

- Spraying a mohair angora sweater with hair spray will keep it from shedding.

- Vanilla or lemon extract will get rid of those black scuff marks on the kitchen floor.

- To keep from falling in a shower slippery with soapsuds, line the shower floor with the slip-proof material you use on shelves. It is porous, dries quickly, won't mildew, and is skid proof.

Miscellaneous Tips

- The bubble wrap used to wrap breakable is useful as an insulator in vents to keep out the cold air.

- Roll bath and face towels to get more into a small space.

- When removing small parts from an item you are repairing, lay a piece of double-sided tape nearby and put the parts on the tape in the same order they are removed.

- Keep your tennis shoes looking new by spraying them with spray starch. Wash when soiled and re-spray.

- In bad weather, place paper grocery bags on the floor of your vehicle to absorb moisture and mud. It saves the carpet and makes cleanup easier.

- Place salt and pepper shakers inside cups or mugs when you are traveling. It keeps them upright and prevents spills.

- To clean a skillet: Lay a paper towel on bottom. Wet towel just enough to get it completely wet. Add a few drops of detergent and then let it stand while you do the rest of the dishes. Grease and food will come right off.

- Keep your vacuum cleaner smelling fresh by crumbling a few bay leaves on the carpet and vacuuming them up. The leaves will give the room and the vacuum a fresh scent.

- Mount a paper-towel rack inside your storage compartment door for any cleanup work while you are outside. Saves running in and out to get it. Place a rubber band on the roll when traveling to keep it from unrolling, or use a clothespin pinned to the side of a few sheets to keep it from unrolling.

- Buy plastic throwaway gloves to wear when you are dumping. They cost very little and will keep your hands clean.

- Do you have to slam your RV doors to close it? Get a tube of wax material, called Door Ease, from auto supply store. Apply it to the striker mechanisms on a regular basis to lubricate the parts.

- Check your battery water every one to two weeks when using the rig and once a month when it is not in use. Batteries that run dry will fail when you need them the most.

Miscellaneous Tips

- Tack a piece of sewing elastic from side to side of a small drawer to keep small bottles (nail polish, etc.) from falling over.

- Use a walker? Take a grocery bag—the kind with handles—and tie one handle to the left arm of the walker and the other handle to the right arm. The bag will remain open in front of you and can be used to carry everything from eyeglasses to tissues.

- Instead of lining kitchen cabinet shelves and drawers with self-adhesive vinyl, cut cardboard to fit the area and cover it with the vinyl. When it is time to clean, remove from the drawer, wash, and then replace.

- Another suggestion is to buy inexpensive place mats and cut them to fit the bottom of drawers.

- Folding chairs with small legs may sink in soft ground or sand. Put a jar lid under each leg to prevent the chair from sinking.

- Keep large plastic bags in your rig or truck. Then can serve as an emergency raincoat.

- After addressing a package with a felt-tip marker, rub a white candle over the writing to seal it and rain won't smudge it.

- If your vehicle is not garaged overnight during cold weather, cover the side-view mirror with a plastic bag held in place with a clothespin. The mirror will be clear in the morning.

- A small paintbrush is perfect for dusting in small places. It works especially well on the car dash and radio.

- Next time you want to put on a decal, spray soapy water on the area, place the decal on the soapy spot, get it straight, then squeeze the water out from under it. When dry, it will stick tight.

- Canvas awnings can be made to look like new by painting with canvas paint. (Available in paint stores.)

- Almost anything can be attached to the walls by using a hot glue gun. To remove, heat the glue with a hair dryer and it will pull away from wall.

- If you need a quick centerpiece, just core an apple, orange, or grapefruit, and then put a candle in the middle.

Hints On Using Source Addresses

by phred Tinseth

Prices change. You send someone $1.98 for a book or catalog and your letter comes back with a request for another dollar. Most businesses will send it anyway.

800 Numbers: If you call a toll free number and can't get through, the number may be discontinued or it may have changed. Make sure you have the correct company name, then call 800-555-1212 and ask for a listing. Many companies have 800 toll-free numbers that are not advertised.

Letters: If you want to ask about a product, type (or print) a concise letter that asks simple, specific questions. Leave room enough for the recipient to jot down answers to your questions and encourage them to do so. If you make things simple for them, an executive or an engineer may personally answer your questions. When you make things easy, your query will not get "lost" (i.e. tossed in the trash).

SASE: *Self Addressed, Stamped Envelope.* There's no better way to insure a prompt reply. If you're writing to ask for something free, like information, it's simple courtesy to include a SASE. Authors get hundreds of letters asking for information. Figure the cost of paper and envelopes, the time needed to answer your letter. address an envelope and add a stamp. Mail that does not include a SASE often gets tossed in the trash if writer is asking for something free.

On the other hand, if you want a brochure or catalog, it indicates you're a buyer. No SASE needed. Again, though, if you want a *prompt* reply, go ahead and send the SASE. You'll be surprised how often some low-level person who just opens the mail will stuff a SASE with all sorts of valuable stuff. So *never* send a dinky little SASE. Send a big, legal-sized SASE.

Do you want a catalog but don't know how much it costs? Send a simple, typed letter asking for the cost of the catalog. Enclose a SASE. Usually, you'll receive a free catalog in a *big* envelope that also returns your SASE.

Editor's Note: phred Tinseth keeps updated source lists on many products. Send $2 for each list to cover postage and printing. Source lists include: General, Inverters, Macerators and Sewer, Buying an RV, Batteries and Electrical Stuff, and Trouble-shooting procedures.

Part 2

Addresses and Phone Numbers of RV Sources

There are many more sources than those listed in this book. If you have found one and think it is good, please send to publisher for inclusion in the next edition of Encyclopedia For RVers.

MOTOR HOME

Airstream Inc (Thor Ind.)
  419 W. Pike St.
  Jackson Center, OH 45334
  (513) 596-6111
  (Class A)

Barth Inc.
  P.O. Box 768
  Milford, IN 46542
  (219) 658-9401
  (Class A)

BBC R.V. Inc.
  R.R. 1, Box 10
  Wakita, OK 73771
  (405) 594-6217
  (Class A--Navette)

Beaver Coaches, Inc.
  20545 Murray Rd.
  Bend, OR 97701
  (503) 389-1144
  (800) 423-2837
  (Class A)

Blue Bird Wanderlodge
  One Wanderlodge Way
  Fort Valley, GA 31030
  (912) 825-2021
  (Class A)

Born Free Inc. (Dodgen Inc.)
  P.O. Box 39
  Humboldt, IA 50548
  (515) 332-3755
  (Mini)

Champion Motor Coach Inc.
  5573 North St.
  Dryden, MI 48428
  (313) 796-2211
  (Class A and Mini)

Coachmen Industries Inc.
  P.O. Box 3300
  Elkhart, IN 46515
  (219) 262-0123
  (Class A and Mini)

Cobra Industries Inc.
  P.O. Box 124
  Goshen, IN 46527
  (219) 534-1418
  (Class A and Mini)

Country Coach Inc.
  P.O. Box 400
  Junction City, OR 97448
  (503) 998-3720
  (Class A)

Travelcraft
  1045 N. Nappanee
  Elkhart, IN 46515
  (219) 264-0202
  (Mini)

Damon Corp.
  52570 Paul Dr.
  Elkhart IN 46514
  (219) 262-2624
  (Class A and Mini)

Firan Motor Coach Inc.
  P.O. Box 482
  Elkhart, IN 46515
  (219) 293-6581
  (Class A and Mini)

Fleetwood Enterprises Inc.
  P.O. Box 7638
  Riverside, CA 92513-7638
  (909) 351-3500
  (Class A)

Foretravel Inc.
  1221 N.W. Stallings Dr.
  Nacogdoches, TX 75961
  (409) 564-8367
  (Class A)

Four Winds Intl. Corp. (Thor)
  P.O. Box 1486
  Elkhart, IN 46515-1486
  (219) 266-1111
  (Class A and Mini)

MOTOR HOME

General Coach (Thor/Canada))
P.O. Box 10
Hensall, ON CN NOM 1X0
(519) 262-2600
Class A and Mini)

Georgie Boy Mfg. Inc.
69950 M-62
Edwardsburg, MI 49112
(800) 521-8733
(616) 663-3415
(Class A)

Go Vacations Inc.
66 Mohawk St.
Brantford, ON CN N3S 2W3
(519) 759-5652
(Mini)

Gulf Stream Coach Inc.
P.O. Box 1005
Nappanee, IN 46550
(219) 773-7761
(Class A and Mini)

Hallcraft RV Industries Inc.
1760 Chicago Ave. Bldg. K
Riverside, CA 92507
(714) 276-1341
(Class A-Chaparral)

Hawkins Motor Coach Inc.
1610 S. Cucamonga Ave.
Ontario, CA 91761
(909) 947-2512
(Class A)

Holiday Rambler Corp.
P.O. Box 465
Wakarusa, IN 46573-0465
(219) 862-7211
(Class A)

Honorbuilt Industries Inc.
P.O. Box 266
Minneapolis, MN 67467
(913) 392-2171
(Class A and Mini)

Intl Vehicles Corp. (Falcon)
P.O. Box 459
Bristol, IN 46507
(219) 848-7686
(Mini)

Jayco Inc.
P.O. Box 460
Middlebury, IN 46540
(219) 825-5861
(Mini)

Lazy Daze Inc.
4303 E. Mission Blvd.
Pomona, CA 91766
(714) 627-1219
(Mini)

Marathon Homes Corp.
P.O. Box 1302
Elkhart, IN 46515
(219) 294-6441
(Mini)

Monoco Coach Corp.
91320 Coburg Ind. Way
Coburg, OR 97408,
(800) 634-0855
(541) 686-8011
(Class A)

Moonlighting Coachworks
1521 Ocean Ave.
Bohemia, NY 11716
(516) 563-8077
(Mini)

National RV Inc. (Dolphin)
3411 N. Perris Blvd.
Perris, CA 92571
(909) 943-6007
(Class A and Mini)

Newmar Corp.
P.O. Box 30
Nappanee, IN 46550
(219) 773-7791
(Class A and Mini)

MOTOR HOME

Odessa Industries Inc.
  2298 Middlebury St.
  Elkhart, IN 46516
  (219) 293-0595
  (Class A)

Okanagan Mfg. (Thor)
  316 Dawson Ave.
  Penticton, BC CN V2A 3N6
  (Mini)

Revcon Motorcoach Inc.
  17422 Pullman
  Irvine, CA 92714
  (714) 955-5340
  (Mini)

Rexhall Industries Inc.
  29449 U.S. 33W.
  Elkhart, IN 46516
  (219) 295-1805
  (Class A)

Safari Motor Coaches Inc.
  P.O. Box 740
  Harrisburg, OR 97446
  (503) 995-8214
  (Class A)

Serro Scotty RV
  450 Arona Rd.
  Irwin, PA 15642
  (412) 863-3407
  (Mini)

Shasta Ind. (Coachmen Inc.)
  P.O. Box 631
  Middlebury, IN 46540
  (219) 825-8555
  (Mini)

Sportscoach of America
  P.O. Box 30
  Middlebury, IN 46540
  (219) 825-8500
  (Class A)

Thor Industries
  419 W. Pike St.
  Jackson Center, OH 45334
  (513) 596-6849
  (Class A and Mini)

Tiffin Motor Homes Inc.
  P.O. Box 596
  Red Bay, AL 35582
  (205) 356-8661
  (Class A and Mini)

Trail Wagons/Chinook
  P.O. Box 2589
  Yakima, WA 98901
  (509) 248-9026
  (Mini)

Triple E Canada Ltd.
  P.O. Box 1230
  Winkler, MB CN R6W 4C4
  (204) 325-4361
  (Class A and Mini)

Vogue by Mitchell
  P.O. Box 339
  Pryor, OK 74362
  (918) 825-7000
  (Bus and Class A)

Winnebago Industries Inc.
  P.O. Box 152
  Forest City, IA 50436
  (515) 582-3535
  (Class A and Mini)

Xplorer Motor Home Div.
  Frank Industries Inc.
  3950 Burnsline Rd.
  Brown City. MI 48416
  (810) 346-2771
  (Class A and van conversion)

Morrisons V.I.P.
  Fresno, CA
  (800) 884-7787
  Coach Slideout conversion specialist

5TH-W and TRAVEL TRAILER

ABI Leisure Prod. (Award)
P.O. Box 208
Dunnville, ON CN N1A 2X1
(905) 774-8891
(5th-W and Travel Trailer)

Airstream Inc (Thor Ind.)
419 W. Pike St.
Jackson Center, OH 45334
(513) 596-6111
(Travel Trailer)

Alfa Leisure Inc.
13501 Fifth St.
Chino, CA 91710
(909) 628-5574
(5th-W and Travel Trailer)

Allen Camper Mfg. Co. Onc.
Rte. 1, Box 16
Allen, OK 74825
(405) 857-2413
(5th-W and Travel Trailer)

American Travel Systems
21746 Buckingham Rd.
Elkhart, IN 46516
(219) 294-2117
(5th-W and Travel Trailer)

Amerigo Corp.
P.O. Box 869
Bristol, IN 46507
(219) 848-7600
(5th-W and Travel Trailer)

Auto-Mate Rec. Prod. Inc.
P.O. Box 831
Los Banos, CA 93635
(209) 826-1521
(5th-W and Travel Trailer)

Avion, Sub./Fleetwood
13737 Industrial Rd.
Omaha, NE 68137
(402) 895-1850
(5th-W and Travel Trailer)

Bigfoot Industries Inc.
3405 -43rd Ave.
Vernon, BC CN V1T 8P5
(604) 549-4222
(5th-W and Travel Trailer)

Carriage Inc.
P.O. Box 246
Millersburg, IN 46543
(219) 642-3622
(5th-W and Travel Trailer)

Casa Villa Inc.
P.O. Box 567
Wakarusa, IN 46573
(219) 862-4531
(5th-W and park models)

Coachmen Industries Inc.
P.O. Box 3300
Elkhart, IN 46515
(219) 262-0123
(5th-W and Travel Trailer)

Cobra Industries Inc.
P.O. Box 124
Goshen, IN 46527
(219) 534-1418
(5th-W and Travel Trailer)

Country Comfort Corp.
21279 Protecta Dr.
Elkhart, IN 46516
(219) 522-3377
(5th-W and Travel Trailer)

Country Villa Inc.
2525 Earren St.
Elkhart, IN 46516
(219) 295-7380
(5th-W and park model)

Craft Products (Travelcraft)
1045 N. Nappanee
Elkhart, IN 46515
(219) 264-0202
(Travel Trailer)

5TH-W and TRAVEL TRAILER

Custom Campers Inc.
    W. 21st St.
    Chanute, KS 66720
    (316) 431-3990
    (5th-W Hitchhiker)

Damon Corp.
    P.O. Box 1107
    Elkhart IN 46514
    (219) 262-2624
    (5th-W and Travel Trailer)

Dutchmen Mfg, Inc. (Thor)
    305 Steury Ave.
    Goshen, IN 46514
    (219) 534-1224
    (5th-W and Travel Trailer)

Excel Trailer Co. Inc.
    5111 Grumman Dr.
    Carson City, NV 89706
    (702) 885-0808
    (5th-W and Travel Trailer)

Fabricated Products Co.
    2049 Piedmont Ave.
    Tripoli, IA 50676
    (319) 882-4409
    (fiberglass Travel Trailer)

Fleetwood Enterprises Inc.
    P.O. Box 7638
    Riverside, CA 92513-7638
    (909) 351-3500
    (5th-W and Travel Trailer)

Franklin Coach Co. Inc.
    P.O. Box 152
    Nappanee, IN 46550
    (219) 773-4106
    (5th-W and Travel Trailer)

General Coach (Div. Thor)
    P.O. Box 10
    Hensall, ON CN NOM 1X0
    (519) 262-2600
    (5th-W and Travel Trailer)

Gulf Stream Coach Inc.
    P.O. Box 1005
    Nappanee, IN 46550
    (219) 773-7761
    (5th-W and Travel Trailer)

Harmar Inc.
    58456 C.R. 3 South
    Elkhart, IN 46517
    (219) 294-1269
    (5th-W and Travel Trailer)

Hi Lo Trailer Co.
    145 Elm St.
    Butler, OH 44822
    (419) 883-3000
    (Travel Trailer)

Holiday Rambler Corp.
    P.O. Box 465
    Wakarusa, IN 46573-0465
    (219) 862-7211
    (5th-W and Travel Trailer)

Homesteader Inc.
    P.O. Box 320
    New Tazewell, TN 37825
    (615) 626-9040
    (5th-W and Travel Trailer)

Honorbuilt Industries Inc.
    P.O. Box 266
    Minneapolis, MN 67467
    (913) 392-2171
    (5th-W)

Horizons Inc.
    2323 N. Jackson
    Junction City, KS 66441
    (913) 238-7575
    (5th-W and Travel Trailer)

Hy-Line Enterprises Inc.
    21674 Beck Dr.
    Elkhart, IN 46516
    (219) 294-1112
    (5th-W and Travel Trailer)

5TH-W and TRAVEL TRAILER

Jayco Inc.
P.O. Box 460
Middlebury, IN 46540
(219) 825-5861
(5th-W and Travel Trailer)

K.Z. Inc./Sportsmen
9720 W. -U.S. 20
Shipshewana, IN 46565
(219) 768-4016
(5th-W and Travel Trailer)

King of the Road
P.O. Box 553
Russell, KS 67665
(913) 483-2138
(5th-W and Travel Trailer)

KIT Mfg. Co.
P.O. Box 990
Caldwell, ID 83606
(208) 454-9291
(5th-W and Travel Trailer)

Lake Capitol Corp. (Komfort)
P.O. Box 68305
Milwaukie, OR 97268
(503) 653-1160
(5th-W and Travel Trailer)

Layton Sub: Skyline Corp.
P.O. Box 2195
Hemet, CA 92546
(909) 925-0401
(5th-W and Travel Trailer)

Marathon Homes Corp.
P.O. Box 1302
Elkhart, IN 46515
(219) 294-6441
(5th-W and Travel Trailer)

Mity-Lite Travel Trailer
400 Farr Shores Dr. 7-E
Hot Springs, AR 71913
(501) 262-4848
(5th-W and Travel Trailer)

Newmar Corp.
P.O. Box 30
Nappanee, IN 46550
(219) 773-7791
(5th-W and Travel Trailer)

Nu-Wa Industries Inc.
P.O. Box 808
Chanute, KS 66720
(316) 431-2088
(5th-W and Travel Trailer)

Okanagan Mfg. (Thor)
316 Dawson Ave.
Penticton, BC CN V2A 3N6
(5th-W)

Peterson Industries Inc. (Excel)
R.R. 2, Box 95
Smith Center, KS 66967
(913) 282-6692
(5th-W and Travel Trailer)

Play-Mor Trailers Inc.
P.O. Box 128
Westphalia, MO 65085
(314) 455-2387
(5th-W and Travel Trailer)

Serro Scotty RV
450 Arona Rd.
Irwin, PA 15642
(412) 863-3407
(5th-W and Travel Trailer)

Shadow Cruiser Inc.
13861 C.R. 4
Bristol, IN 46507
(219) 825-1000
(5th-W and Travel Trailer)

Shasta Ind. (Coachmen Inc.)
P.O. Box 631
Middlebury, IN 46540
(219) 825-8555
(5th-W and Travel Trailer)

5TH-W and TRAVEL TRAILER

Silver Star RV (Silver Streak)
4741 Murietta St.
Chino, CA 91710
(909) 591-0416
(5th-W and Travel Trailer)

Skamper Corp.
P.O. Box 338
Bristol, IN 46507
(219) 848-7411
(5th-W and Travel Trailer)

Skyline Corp.
P.O. Box 743
Elkhart, IN 46515
(219) 294-6521
(5th-W and Travel Trailer)

Starcraft RV Inc. (Jayco Inc.)
P.O. Box 458
Topeka, IN 46571
(219) 593-2550
(5th-W and Travel Trailer)

Sun-Lite Inc.
P.O. Box 517
Bristol, IN 46507
(219) 295-5410
(small Travel Trailer)

Sunline Coach Co.
245 S. Muddy Creek Rd.
Denver, PA 17517
(717) 336-2858
(5th-W and Travel Trailer)

Sunnybrook RV Inc.
11756 C.R. 14
Middlebury, IN 46540
(219) 825-5250
(5th-W and Travel Trailer)

Teton Intl/B&B Homes
P.O. Box 2349
Mills, WY 82644
(307) 265-9594
(5th-W with super slides)

Thor Industries
419 W. Pike St.
Jackson Center, OH 45334
(513) 596-6849
(5th-W and Travel Trailer)

TrailManor Inc.
P.O. Box 130
Lake City, TN 37769
(615) 426-7426
(Travel Trailer)

Travel Line Enterprises Inc.
25876 Miner Rd.
Elkhart, IN 46514
(219) 264-3127
(5th-W and Travel Trailer)

Travel Supreme Inc.
P.O. Box 610
Wakarusa, IN 46573
(219) 862-4484
(5th-W and Travel Trailer)

Veri-Lite Inc.
P.O. Box 339
Elkhart, IN 46515
(219) 295-8318
(5th-W and Travel Trailer)

Weekend Warrior Trailers
1614 E. Holt Ave.
Ontario, CA 91761
(909) 983-9914
(5th-W and Travel Trailer)

Western R.V.
P.O. Box 9547
Yakima, WA 98903
(509) 457-4133

PARK MODEL

Bayside RV
2300 Napoleon
Freemont, OH 43420
(419) 334-5678

Casa Villa Inc.
P.O. Box 567
Wakarusa, IN 46573
(219) 862-4531

Chariot Eagle Inc.
931 N.W. 37th Ave.
Ocala, FL 34475
(904) 629-7007

Estate Mfg. Inc.
22617 Pine Creek Road
Elkhart, IN 46516
(219) 295-3682

Fairmont Homes Inc.
P.O. Box 27
Nappanee, IN 46550
(219) 773-7941

General Coach
Div/Thor Ind. Inc.
P.O. Box 10
Hensall, ON
CN N0M 1X0
(519) 262-2600

Glendale Rec. Veh. Inc.
444 N. Nappanee #204
Elkhart, IN 46514
(219) 293-7376

Homette Corp.
Sub/Skyline Corp.
P.O. Box 2648
Ocala, FL 32678
(904) 622-2777

Hy-Line Enterprises Inc.
21674 Beck Dr.
Elkhart, IN 46516
(219) 294-1112

Kropf Mfg. Co. Inc.
P.O. Box 30
Goshen, IN 46526
(219) 533-2171

Layton Travel Trailer
Sub./Skyline Corp.
P.O. Box 2195
Hemet, CA 92546
(909) 925-0401

Lee Ent. Mfg. Co. Inc.
25883 N. Park Ave.
Elkhart, IN 46514
(219) 262-1543

Nomad Travel Trailers
77 Horseshoe Dr.
Leola, PA 17546
(717) 656-2111

Parkwest Industries Inc.
644 W. McKellips Rd.
Mesa, AZ 85201
(602) 649-9770

Snoke & Son Mfg. Inc.
2415 2nd Ave. E.
Bradenton, FL 34208
(813) 645-7712

Travel Line Ent. Inc.
25876 Miner Rd.
Elkhart, IN 46514
(219) 264-3127

Wheel House Structures Inc.
P.O. Box 928
Haleyville, AL 35565
(205) 486-8475

Woodland Park, Inc.
P.O. Box 1309
Middlebury, IN 46540
(219) 825-2104

BUS CONVERSIONS

Angola Coach, Inc.
P.O. Box 301
Angola, IN 46703
(219) 665-6361

Crown Custom Coach
5433 Milton Pkw
Rosemont, IL 60016
(708) 678-4800

Custom Coach Corp.
1400 Dublin Road
Columbus, OH 43215
(800)-852-5979

El Dorado National Co.
13900 Sycamore Way
Chino, CA 91710
(800) 682-4100

Hausman Bus Sales & Parts
10 East Golf Road
Des Plaines, IL 60016-2291
(800) 428-7626

Liberty Coach Inc.
1400 Morrow Ave N.
N. Chicago, IL 60064
(800) 332-9877

Marathon Coach, Inc.
91333 Coburg Industrial Way
Coburg, OR 97408
(800) 234-9991

Turtle Top
67895 Industrial Dr.
New Paris, IN 46553
(219) 831-5680

ACCESSORIES for the HANDICAPPED

Alternative Mobility, Inc.
28244 Clay St.
Elkhart, IN 46517
(219) 293-0367

B & W Handicap Equip.
P.O. Box 1075
Fayettville, GA 30214
(404) 460-1909
(404) 460-1677
(hand controls/wc lifts)

Braun Corporation
P.O. Box 310
Winamac, IN 46996
(219) 946-6157
(Lifts for RVs)

First Care Service/Supplies
and respiratory services
122 N. Main
Pratt, Kansas 67124
(316) 672-6429

Handicap Services, Inc.
1820 Kings Hwy
Shreveport, LA 71103
(318) 226-0935

Handicapped Driving Systems
12251 Nicollet Ave S.
Burnsville, MN 55337
(612) 894-1914

Handicapped Driving Aids
3990 Second Street
Wayne, MI 48184
(313) 595-4400
(specialized equipment)

Handi Ramp
P.O. Box 745
Mundelein, IL 60060
(800) 876-7267
(ramps and tracks)

Leisure Lift
1800 Merriam Lane
Kansas City, Kansas 66106
(800) 255-0285
(self-help stand-up chairs)

Ricon Corp.
12450 Montague St.
Pacoloma, CA 91331
(800) 322-2884
(wheelchair lifts)

CUSTOMIZE FOR HANDICAPPED

Access Industries Inc..
2509 Summer Ave.
Memphis, TN 38112
(901) 323-5438

Ahnafield Corp.
3219 W. Washington St.
Indianapolis, IN 46222
(317) 636-8061

Alternative Mobility, Inc.
(Braun product line)
28244 Clay St.
Elkhart, IN 46517
(219) 293-0367

Barth, Inc.
P.O. Box 768
Milford, IN 46542
(800) 348-5088

B & W Handicap Equip.
P.O. Box 1075
Fayette, GA 39214
(404) 460-1909

Chrysler Corp.
(Resource Center)
1220 Rankin St.
Troy, MI 48083-6004
(800) 255-9877

Coachman Ind. Corp.
27251 Hune St.
Brownsville, OR 97327
(503) 466-5131
(specialty vehicles)

Diamond Coach Corp.
2300 West Fourth Street
Oswego, KS 67356
(316) 795-2191
(buses and vans only)

Foretravel of Texas, Inc.
1221 N.W. Stallings Drive
Nacogdoches, TX 75964
(409) 564-8367
(Equip for disabled)

GM Mobility Assis. Center
P.O. Box 9011
Detroit, MI 48202
(800) 323-9935

Honorbuilt, Inc.
1200 West 10th
Minneapolis, KS 67467
(913) 392-2171

J&R Camper & Trailer Rep.
7910 Aldrich Ave. N.
Brooklyn Park, MN 55444
(612) 588-9333

Monmouth Custom Vans
5105 Rires 33/34
Farmingdale, NJ 07727
(908) 919-1444
(special supplies/equip.)

Ricon Corporation
12450 Montague St.
Pacoima, CA 91331
(800) 322-2884
(818) 899-7588
(Handicap units)

RoadRunner Vans Inc.
805 S. Sherman St.
Richardson, TX 75081
(214) 783-8155
(specialty vehicles)

Senator Buses/ Supreme Corp.
Goshen, IN 46526
(219) 642-4888
(handicap lifts)

Travel Units, Inc.
28748 Holiday Place
Elkhart, IN 46515
(219) 293-8785
(Specialize in trailers)

MOTOR HOME CHASSIS

Chevrolet Motor Division
  30007 Van Dyke, Rm 246-06
  Warren, MI 48090
  (313) 492-5400
  (810) 492-5403

Ford Motor Co, Div,
  P.O. Box 43306
  Detroit, MI 48243
  (313) 446-4124

Freightliner Custom Chassis
  552 Hyatt St.
  Gaffney, SC 29341
  (803) 487-1700

Gillig Corporation
  Box 3008
  Hayward. CA 94540
  (510) 785-1500
  (510) 264-5013

Oshkosh Chassis Center
  552 Hyatt St.
  Gaffney,SC 29341
  (414) 235-9150

Sparton Motors, Inc.
  1000 Reynolds
  Charlotte, MI 48813
  (517) 543-6400

DIESEL ENGINES

Caterpillar, Inc.
  P.O. Box 610
  Mossville, IL 61552
  (309) 578-7433

Cummins Engine Co.
  Box 3005
  Columbus, IN 47202
  (812) 377-3688

Cummins Power Sys. Inc.
  2727 Ford Rd.
  Bristol, PA 19007
  (215) 785-6005

Detroit Diesel Corp.
  13400 Outer Drive West
  Detroit, MI 48239
  (313) 592-5292

TRANSMISSIONS

Allison Transmission
  P.O. Box 894 PF 8
  Indianapolis, IN 46206
  (317) 242-3132
  (317) 242-0225

Eaton Corp.
  P.O. Box 4013
  Kalamazoo, MI 49003
  (616) 342-3000

John Kilgore Transmissions
  412 S. San Fernando
  Burbank, CA 91502
  (818) 843-7180

Tekonsha Engineering Co.
  537 N. Church St.
  Tekonsha, MI 49092
  (517) 767-4142

TURBO CHARGERS

Advanced Turbo Systems
  P.O. Box 57547
  Murray, UT 84107
  (800) 68 TURBO
  (801) 263-0900

Hypermax Engineering Inc.
  255 East Route 72
  Gilberts, IL 60136
  (708) 428-5655

AIR CONDITIONING

Atwood Mobile Products
    4750 Hiawatha Drive
    Rockford, IL 61103
    (815) 877-5700

Coleman Company, Inc
    3110 N. Mead
    Wichita, KS 67219
    (316) 832-6532

Combo Air Mfg, Inc.
    1172 N.W. 51st Street
    Ft. Lauderdale, FL 33309
    (305) 491-5151

Dometic Corp (Dua-Therm)
    P.O. Box 490
    Elkhart, IN 46515
    (219) 294-2511

Emerson Quiet Kool Corp.
    25416 CR 6 East
    Elkhart, IN 46514
    (219) 262-1787

Frigi-Cool, Inc.
    P.O. Box 116968
    Carrollton, TX 75011
    (800) 527-0839

ANTENNAS

Barker Mfg. Company
    730 E. Michigan Avenue
    Battle Creek MI 49017
    (616) 965-2371

Carter Shades, Inc.
    18475 Olympic Ave. South
    Seattle, WA 98188
    (206) 251-5203

Van Ordt, Inc.
    10875 S. Grand Ave.
    Ontario. CA 91761
    (714) 628-4791

Winegard Company
    3000 Kirkwood Street
    Burlington, IA 52601
    (319) 754-0621

AWNINGS

Awnings by Omni Inc.
    7234 Overland Rd.
    Orlando, FL 32810
    (407) 299-4950

Carefree of Colorado
    2145 W. 6th
    Broomfield, CO 80020
    (303) 469-3324

Carter Shades, Inc.
    18475 Olympic Ave, South
    Seattle, WA 98188
    (206) 368-8881
    (206) 251-5203

Faulkner Mfg (& Coleman)
    180 Charles Street
    Malden, MA 02148
    (800) 677-7739
    (617) 322-7300

Zip Dee Inc.
    96 Crossen Avenue
    Elk Grove Village, IL 60007
    (708) 437-0980
    (800) 338-2378

BATTERY CHARGERS

Heart Interface Corp.
  21440 -68th Ave.
  Kent, WA 98032
  (206) 872-7225

Kool-O-Matic Corp.
  P. O. Box 310
  Niles, MI 49120
  (616) 683-2600

Sunlight Energy Corp.
  4411 W. Echo Lane
  Glendale, AZ 85302
  (800) 338-1781
  (602) 934-6492

Todd Engineering Sales, Inc.
  3282 E. Hemisphere Loop #154
  Tucson, AZ 85706
  (602) 889-9333

Trace Engineering
  5916- 195th St. N.E.
  Arlington, WA 98223
  (360) 435-8826

TRUEcharge
  (by STATPOWER)
  (800) 668-0003

CONVERTERS

Koolatron Corporation
  27 Catharine Ave
  Brantford, Ontario N3T 1X5
  (519) 756-3950

Onan Corporation
  1400 -73rd Ave NE
  Minneapolis, MN 55432
  (612) 574-5000

Suburban Mfg Co.
  P.O. Box 399
  Dayton,TN 37321
  (615) 775-2131
  (also sells heaters)

EVAPORATIVE COOLERS: 12-VOLT

Dometic Corporation
  P.O. Box 490
  Elkhart, IN 46515
  (800) 544-4881

RECAIR
Redwood Engineering Corp
  26690 Wagonwheel Drive
  Pioneer, CA 95666
  (209) 295-7556

FREEZERS

Norcold Dirs. (Stolle Corp.)
  P. O. Box 180
  Sidney, OH 43635
  (513) 498-6781
  (reefers and portable freezer)

NOVA KOOL
Box 80749, 5950 Imperial St.
Burnaby, BC, Canada V5H 3Y1
(order from Backwoods Solar)
(208) 263-4290

Sun Frost
  Box 1101
  Arcata, CA 95521
  (707) 822-9095
  (12-volt compressor
   operated not propane)

FURNACES

Atwood Mobile Products
    4750 Hiawatha Dr.
    Rockford, IL 61103
    (815) 877-5700

Bergstrom Mfg Co
    P.O. Box 6007
    Rockford, IL 61125
    (815) 874-7821

Dometic Sales Corporation
    P. O. Box 490
    Elkhart, IN 46515
    (800) 544-4881
    (219) 294-2511

Suburban Mfg Co, Inc.
    P.O. Box 399
    Dayton, TN 37321
    (615) 775-2131

U.S. Catalytic Corporation
    870 Napa Valley Corp. Way
    Suite K
    Napa, CA 94558-6249
    (707) 255-4181
    (Olympian catalytic heater)

FURNITURE

A.M. Enterprises
    14145 SE 16th Ct.
    Summerfield, FL 34491-2009
    (904) 245-1577

Braddt Hall Associates
    601 W. 400 North
    Angola, IN 46703
    (219) 825-2664

Crown Custom Coach
    5433 Milton Parkway
    Rosemont, IL 60016
    (708) 678-4800

Custom Wood Products, Inc.
    P.O. Box 925
    Wakanusa, IN 46573
    (219) 862-2815

Hi-Lo Table Mfg. Inc.
    P.O. Box 888
    Chanute, KS 66720
    (316) 431-7140

Kinder Mfg. Co.
    P.O. Box 1207
    Elkhart, IN 46515
    (219) 293-3531
    (upholstered furniture
    and cushions)

KWIKEE Products Co.
    2947 State Hwy 38
    Drain, OR 97435
    (503) 836-2126
    (pull-out/slide-out trays)

Mastercraft, Inc.
    P.O. Box 326
    Shipshewana, IN 46565
    (recliner, barrel chair, sofa etc.)

Preferred Custom Concepts
    P.O. Box 0069
    Crandall, TX 75114
    (214) 472-6600
    (floor & overhead consoles)

RV Interiors
    12205 S. Gilbert Rd.
    Gilbert, AZ 85296
    (602) 926-2720

Villa Hallmark
    502 E. Julianna St.
    Anaheim, CA 92801
    (714) 535-7272

Westlake, Inc.
    40 N. Water St.
    Lititz, PA 17543
    (717) 626-0272

GENERATORS

Honda /Western Distrib.
   P.O. Box 44548
   Tacoma, WA 98444
   (206) 539-0381

Hicklin Power Systems
   5303 NW 111th Dr.
   Grimes, IA 50111-8732
   (515) 986-9557
   (Honda parts & service)

Generac Corporation
   P. O. Box 8
   Waukesha, WI 53187
   (414) 544-4811

Kohler Company
   444 Highland Drive
   Kohler, WI 53044
   (414) 565-3381

Onan Corporation
   1400 - 73rd Avenue N.E.
   Minneapolis, MN 55432
   (612) 574-5911
   (800) 888-ONAN

T.A.W. Power Systems
   440 S. 78th St.
   Tampa, FL 33619
   (800) 456-9449
   (Kohler generators and parts,
   service, repair)

Wrico International
   P.O. Box 41555
   Eugene, OR 97404
   (503) 689-4245
   (Diesel generators)

INVERTERS

Best Power Technology
   P.O. Box 280
   Necedah, WI 54646
   (608) 565-7200
   (800) 356-5794

Cummins Power Sys. Inc.
   2727 Ford Rd.
   Bristol, PA 19007
   (215) 785-6005
   (Redline inverters)

Heart Interface Corporation
   21440- 68th Ave.
   Kent, WA 98032
   (800) 446-6180
   (206) 872-7225

Kohler Company
   444 Highland Dr.
   Kohler, WI 53044
   (414) 565-3381

Statpower Technical Corp.
   7725 Lougheed Hwy
   Burnaby, BC,
   Canada V5A 4V8
   (800) 668-0003

Trace Engineering
   5916 -195th N.E.
   Arlington, WA 98223
   (206) 435-2229

Tripp Lite
   500 N. Orleans
   Chicago, IL 60610
   (312) 755-8741

Vanner Weldon, Inc.
   4282 Reynolds Dr.
   Hilliard, OH 43026
   (614) 771--2718
   (also related products)

JACKS/LEVELING/SUSPENSION SYSTEMS

Air-Ax
Cty Rd 1 & 18, Box 64
Edgerton, MN 56128
(507) 442-8201
(air suspension system)

B.F. Goodrich
6061 Goodrich Blvd.
Jacksonville, FL 32226
(905) 757-3660
(suspension system)

Barker Mfg. Co.
730 E. Michigan Ave.
Battle Creek, MI 49017
(616) 965-2371
(jacks/levels)

Holloway Mfg. Corp.
100 Arlington Dr.
Granite City, IL 62040
(618) 797-0365

HWH Corporation
R.R. # 1
Moscow, II 52760
(319) 724-3396
(hydraulic leveling system)

ipd Company, Inc.
11744 N.E. Ainsworth Circle
Portland, OR 97220
(800) 444-6486

Jet Company, Inc.
1303 N. 13th St.
Humboldt, IA 50548
(800) 332-3117

MAI (Mobile Acces. Inc.)
4575 Carter Court
Chino, CA 91710
(909) 590-1087

MOR/ryde, Inc.
P.O. Box 579
Elkhart, IN 46515
(219) 293-1581
(rubber suspension system)

Norco Industries, Inc.
(Bal Products Division)
365 West Victoria Street
Compton, CA 90220
(800) 347-2232
(213) 636-1176

Quality Coach, Inc.
20 Dowling Drive
Ridgefield, CT 06877
(203) 438-3122

Quadra Mfg., Inc.
(Quadra-EZE)
P.O. Box 536
White Pigeon, MI 49099
(616) 483-9364

Roadmaster Inc.
5602 N.E. Skyport Way
Portland, OR 97218
(503) 288-9898
(tow bars/towing system)

RVA Company
320 N. Market Place
Escondido, CA 92029
(619) 746-5732
(jacks/leveling)

Steer Safe Inc.
P.O. Box 149
Deming, NM 88031
(505) 546-8894
(stablizers)

LIGHTS

(Quartz-Halogen lamps)

A.S.E.
 6965 El Camino Real
 Carlsbad, CA 92009
 (619) 438-0844

Backwoods Solar Electric
 8530 Rapid Lightning Cr. Rd.
 Sandpoint, ID 83864
 (208) 263-4290

Fluorescent

(REC) Thin-Light Corp.
 530 Constitution Avenue
 Camarillo, CA 93012
 (805) 987-5021

Tek Tron Enterprises, Inc.
 3122 W. Alpine Ave.
 Santa Ana, CA 92704
 (send for list)

MACERATOR PUMP

ITT Jabsco
 P.O. Box 2158
 Costa Mesa, CA 92626-2158
 (714) 545-8251
 (call for nearest dealer)

Post Marine Supply
 111 Cedar Street
 New Rochelle, NY 10801
 (800) YACHTER, for catalog
 (Jabsco & Johnson macerators)

West Marine
 Box 50050
 Watsonville, CA 95077-5050
 (800) 538-0775
 (sells Jabsco and Johnson
 macerator pumps)

MIRRORS/MONITOR SYSTEMS

Global World Corp.
 216 Summerwood Trail
 Maitland, FL 32751
 (407) 339-1273

Intec Video Systems, Inc.
 23301 Vista Grande
 Laguna Hills, CA 92653
 (800) 468-3254
 (714) 859-3800

Mark's Products, Inc.
 RearView Vision
 RD #1 Box 303
 Howard, PA 16841
 (814) 355-5092

Ramco Engineering, Inc.
 2019 W. Lusher Ave.
 Elkhart, IN 46517
 (219) 294-7691

Richlund Sales
 75695 Hwy. 1053
 Kentwood, LA 70444
 (504) 229-4956
 (rear vision camera)

Sure View Inc .
 1337 N. Meridan Street
 Wichita, KS 67203
 (316) 945-0851

Velvac Inc.
 2900 S. 160th Street
 New Berlin, WI 53151
 (414) 786-0700

Wheel Masters
 P.O. Box 60910
 Reno, NV 89506
 (702) 972-7888

OVERDRIVE/UNDERDRIVE

Eric's RV
275 S. 7th Ave.
Sequim, WA 98382
(800) 488-3697

Gear Vendors, Inc.
1717 N. Magnolia Ave.
El Cajon, CA 92020-1243
Fax: 619-562-1186

McBride's Serv & Supply
13788 Oaks Avenue
Chino, CA 91710
(800) 421-7788
(714) 627-7566

Mitchell Gear Splitter
100 W. North St.
Healdsburg, CA 95448

PERFORMANCE CENTERS & PRODUCTS

ACCU Power Products
P.O. Box 496
Marshall, MI 49068
(616) 789-0144

Al Carrots Performance RV
1343 Captain Shreve Dr.
Shreveport, LA 71105
(318) 865-2886

ALH Repair & Alignment
1525 Dr. Bramblett Rd.
Cumming, GA 30130
(404) 887-0220

Eric's RV Performance Center
275 S. 7th Ave.
Sequim, WA 98382
(800) 488-3697

Henderson's Line-up
417 SW Marion Lane
Grants Pass, OR 97527
(800) 245-8309
(503) 479-2882

Hyperteck
1910 Thomas Rd.
Memphis, TN 38134
(901) 382-8888
(power chips/modules)

Jardine Performance Exhaust
P.O. Box 8488
Jackson Hole, WY 83011
(800) 934-3569

MAI Mobile Accessories, Inc.
4575 Carter Ct.
Chino, CA 91710
(909) 590-1087

McBride's Serv. & Supply
13788 Oaks Avenue
Chino, CA 91710
(800) 421-7788
(714) 627-7566

Mountain Tamer by
Decelomatic Corp.
4837 E. Indian School Rd.
Phoenix, AZ 85018
(602) 956-8200
(compression/ braking)

R & E Racing
44533 N. Sierra Hwy.
Lancaster, CA 93534
(800-776-6792 (outside CA)
(805) 948-7622 (In CA)

RV Performance Connection
930A Calle Negocio
San Clemente, CA 92673
(714) 366-9590

STC RV Performance Center
12464 McCann Dr.
Santa Fe Springs, CA 90670
(310) 944-3694

PICKUP ACCESSORIES

Advanced Technology Corp.
101 N. Eagle St.
Geneva, OH 44041
(216) 466-4671
(wiring harness)

Auxiliary Fuel Tanks
1444 Fortress St.
Chico, CA 95926
(800) 826- 5776 for catalog
(916) 893-5209

Continental Accessories, Inc.
P. O. Box 617
Sturgis, MI 49091
(800) 253-2001
(616) 651-1741

Creative Industries
Box 248
Kenmore, ND 58746
(800) 543-1218
(storage boxes)

Davidson Enterprises
7109 W. Palo Verde Ave.
Peoria, AZ 85345
(800) 878-8581
(5-W wind deflector)

Kwikee Products Co.
2947 State Hwy 38
Drain, OR 97435
(503) 836-2126
(super slide etc.)

Highway Products Inc.
6241 Crater Lake Hwy
Central Point, OR 97502
(800) 866-5269
(storage box)

ITTCO Sales Co. Inc.
181 Remington Blvd.
Ronkonkoma, NY 11779
(910) 768-6748
(air deflectors)

LMI Welding, Inc.
Box 772
Cut Bank, MT 59427
(406) 337-3021
(800) 345-5623
(seat kit for supercab)

Penda Corporation
2344 W. Wisconsin St.
Portage, WI 53901-0449
(800) 356-7704
(800) 362-7611 (WI)
(PU bedliners)

Row Enterprises
20227 Charlanne Dr.
Redding, CA 96002
(916) 222-6176

R.P.M. ECONO Tanks
13211 Bee St.
Dallas, TX 75234
(214) 247-6881
(extra tank/tool box combo)

Transfer Flow, Inc.
200 Ryan Ave.
Chico, CA 95926
(800) 826-5776
(916) 893-5209
(auxiliary fuel tank)

Wayne Tire & Wheel
P.O. Box 716
White Pigeon, MI 49099
(616) 483-9677

Wheel Masters Inc.
P.O. Box 60910
Reno, NV 89506
(800) 325-9484

Wings
3720 Omec Circle
Rancho Cordova, CA 95670
(800) 634-7757
(storage box)

RACKS/RAILS/RAMPS

Hike-a-Bike, Inc
   2706 S. Willow Ave.
   Fresno, CA 93725
   (800) 541-4453 (USA)
   (rack carries 2 to 4 bikes)

ITTCO Sales Co. Inc.
   181 Remington Blvd.
   Ronkonkoma, NY 11779
   (910) 768-6748
   (roof racks)

Perrycroft Inc.
   2920 Griffith Rd.
   Winston-Salem, NC 27103
   (910) 768-6748

RhinoRamps
   99 S. Cameron St.
   Harrisburg, PA 17101
   (800) 283-6188
   (ramps)

Rola Roof Racks Intl Inc
2121 Cloverfield Blvd
Santa Monica, CA 90404
(310) 474-8885

Stromberg Carlson Products Inc.
225 E. 16th St.
Traverse City, MI 49684
(616) 947-8600

REFRIGERATORS

Coleman Company
   3110 North Mead
   Wichita, KS 67219
   (316) 832-6532

Dometic Sales Corporation
   P. O. Box 490
   Elkhart, IN 46515
   (800) 544-4881
   (219) 463-4858
   (for service mechanic)

Ford RV Refrig. Service Inc.
   1749 Big Bear Hwy.
   Benton, KY 42025
   (502) 354-9239
   (rebuilt RV refrig. & parts)

Magic Chief
   740 King Edward Ave.
   Cleveland, TN 37311

(615) 472-3371

Norcold Dir. (Stolle Corp.)
   P. O. Box 180
   Sidney, OH 43635
   (513) 498-6778
   (reefers and portable freezer)

Nova Kool Mfg (Solar powered)
   Box 80749, 5950 Imperial St.
   Burnaby, BC, Canada V5H 3Y1
   U.S. mail order dealer is
   "Backwoods Solar"
   (also kits for self-installation)

Servel (by Dometic)
   (800) 438-5346
   or (800) 544-4881

Sibir USA Ltd.
   53105 Marina Drive
   Elkhart, IN 46514
   Fax: 219-264-4777

Sun Frost (12-volt)
   Box 1101
   Arcata, CA 95521
   (707) 822-9095

REPAIR PARTS AND SPECIALIZED SUPPLIES

All Seasons RV Appliance
P.O. Box 456
Elkhart, IN 46515
(800) 344-0673
(parts and service)

ASI Distributors
107 N. Main
Tonganoxie, KS 66086
(913) 845-2700
(appliance repair parts)

Centroid Products
2104A Hibiscus Dr.
Edgewater, FL 32032
(904) 423-3574
(probes & tank meters)

DTI RV Appliance Parts
Box 286
Middlebury, IN 46540
(800) 289-0919

Howell's RV Appliance Repair
1162 Greenfield Dr.
El Cajon, CA 92021
(619) 441-0066

Medical Equipment Co.
106 Quigley Blvd.
New Castle, DE 19720
(800) 322-3300
(All types medical equipment)

Midwest Sales & Svc. Inc.
P.O. Box 1020
South Bend, IN 46624
(800) 772-7262
(electronics)

MITO
P.O. Box 1663
Elkhart, IN 46515
(219) 295-2441
(electronics)

Northwest Distributors
412 E. Evans Dr.
Tidewater, OR 97390
(503) 528-7200

Order Desk (The)
1221 Belfair Dr.
Pinole, CA 94564
(800) 526-2066
(consoles, accessories)

Post Marine Supply
111 Cedar St.
New Rochelle, NY 10801
(800) YACHTER
(patching materials and more)

Richlund Sales
75695 Hwy. 1053
Kentwood, LA 70444
(504) 229-4956
(icemaker, compactor etc.)

Royal Appliance Mfg. Co.
650-Alpha Dr.
Cleveland, OH 44143
(800) 321-1134
(Dirt Devil vacuum cleaner)

RV Parts to Go
Sacramento, CA
(800) 563-3916

Shelter Components
P.O. Box 4026
Elkhart, IN 46515
(219) 262-4541
(inside & outside products)

Starline Products
1300 Charlestown Ind. Dr.
St. Charles, MO 63367
(800) 362-0937
(large variety)

West Marine
Box 50050
Watsonville, CA 95077-5050
(800) 538-0775
(patching materials and more)

Wrangler Power Products, Inc.
P.O. Box 12109
Prescott, AZ 86304
(800) 999-2616

ROOF COATINGS

Alpha, Inc.
  5120 Beck Dr.
  Elkhart, IN 46516
  (219) 295-5206

Co-Fair Corp.
  6600 N. Lincoln, #310
  Lincolnwood, IL 60645
  (708) 673-8131

Kool Seal Inc.
  1499 Enterprise Pkw
  Twinsburg, OH 44087
  (216) 425-4717

Plastic Coatings
  P.O. Box 1068
  St. Abans, WV 25177
  (304) 755-9151

Protective Coatings Inc.
  1602 Blackwood Ave.
  Fort Wayne, IN 46803
  (800) 992-8299
  (219) 424-2900

SAFETY/SECURITY SYSTEMS FOR RV

Add-A-Beep
  Proven Items, inc
  6163 Burgoyne
  Houston, TX 77057
  (713) 782-5784
  (Signal beeper warning)

Fat Socks USA
  P.O. Box 2972
  Hemet, CA
  (backup w/solar)

Hana Engineering Inc.
  6820 Orangethorpe Ave. #B
  Buena Park, CA 90620
  (714) 562-0150

Harper's
  74140 El Paseo, Ste. 227
  Palm Desert, CA 92260
  (gas sniffer system)

Land & Sea Yacht Supplies
  3326 Fir Ave.
  Alameda, CA 94502
  (510) 521-5606

NoBi Corp.
  2506 Middlebury St.
  Elkhart, IN 46516
  (219) 295-5765

Touchtronics, Inc.
  57315 Nagy Dr.
  Elkhart, IN 46517
  (219) 294-2570

Trekmate Security
  5085 Caesena Way
  Oceanside, CA 92056
  (619) 941-3444

SATELLITE SYSTEMS

Barker Mfg. Company
   730 E. Michigan Avenue
   Battle Creek, MI 49016
   (616) 965-2371

Bestmade RV Satellites
   2356 South Sarah
   Fresno, CA 93706
   (209) 266-1043
   (800) 262-1044

Moto Satellite
   1805 East 3050 South
   Windell, ID 8335
   (800) 247-7486

Precision RV Systems
   14520 E. Ashlan Ave.
   Sanger, CA 93657
   (209) 275-1780

Travel-Sat/E.L. Carlson Co.
   P.O. Box 11091
   Palm Desert, CA 92255
   (619) 568-0666
   (mfg of tTravel-Sat)

Winegard Company
   3000 Kirkwood Street
   Burlington, IA 52601-2000
   (319) 754-0600

SCREEN ROOMS

Modular Rooms Inc.
   3504 Century Blvd.
   Lakeport, FL 33811
   (800) 880-4397
   (813) 647-5045

RV Screen Room
   3450\Columbia
   White Hall, PA 18052
   (800) 647-4664

SOLAR *see page 130-131*

STEERING SYSTEMS/ STABILIZER

E Tip, Inc.
   PO Box 571
   Addison, IL 60101
   (312) 530-8393

Federal-Mogul Corp.
   P.O. Box 1966
   Detroit, MI 48235
   (810) 354-7700

McCoy Bros. Group Inc.
   9400 -7th St.
   Rancho Cucamonga, CA 91730
   (909) 466-5655

Safe-T-Plus
   2150 Moreland Ave. S.E.
   Atlanta, GA 30315
   (800) 872-7233
   (404) 622-1341

Steer Safe, Inc.
   Box 149
   Deming, NM 88031
   (800) 845-5504

United Safety Apparatus Inc.
   2150 Moreland Ave.
   Atlanta, GA 30315
   (404) 622-1341

SWAY CONTROLS

Draw-Tite Inc.
  40500 Van Born Rd.
  Canton, MI 48188
  (313) 722-7800

Eaz-Lift Spring Corp.
  P.O. Box 489
  Sun Valley, CA 91353
  (818) 768-5880

McCoy Bros. Group Inc.
  9400 -7th St.
  Rancho Cucamonga, CA 91730
  (909) 466-5655

Quality S Manufacturing
  P.O. Box 29310
  Phoenix, AZ 85019
  (800) 521-8181

TOILETS & RELATED PRODUCTS

ECO-SAVE (JWH)
  Box 195
  Santa Rosa, CA 95402
  (800) 950-9666
  (707) 579-0643
  (safe toilet chemical)

JAECO
  12854 Florence Ave.
  Santa Fe Springs, CA 90670
  (800) 944-1959
  (310) 946-2340
  (odor-free toilet)

Jiffy Line Hose Support
  P.O. Box 13821
  S. Lake Tahoe, CA 95702
  (sewer connectors & supports)

Microphor, Inc.
  P.O. Box 1460
  Willits, CA 95490
  (800) 358-8280
  (707) 459-5563
  (water activated/china)

Research Products/Blankenship
  2639 Andjon
  Dallas, TX 75220
  (800) 527-5551
  (Incinolet electric toilet)

SeaLand Technology Inc.
  P.O. Box 38
  Big Prairie, OH 44611
  (800) 321-9886
  (216) 496-3211

Thetford Corporation
  P.O. Box 1285
  Ann Arbor, MI 48106
  (313) 769-6000
  (800) 521-3032

Wolfe & Companies
  P.O. Box 2143
  Arvada, CO 80001
  (303) 425-5709
  (toiler chemicals)

WARNING

Do not use toilet chemicals that contain formaldehyde. It can destroy campround septic systems. Good brands of toilet chemicals include **Plumb John, Always Fresh** (available at RV stores) and **ECO-SAVE.** (Yeast works, but can gum up valves.)

SOLAR AND 12V APPLIANCES

Alternative Energy Engineering
Box 339
Redway, CA 95560
(800) 777-6609
$4 design guide and catalog. Reasonable prices.

Ample Power Company
1150 NW 52nd St.
Seattle, WA 98017
Orders (800) 541-7789
Tech Info (206) 789-4743

Backwoods Solar Electric Systems
Steve Willey
8530 Rapid Lightning Creek Rd.
Sandpoint, ID 83864
(208) 263-4290
Catalog and Planning Guide $4.

FlowLight Solar Power
Windy Dankoff
Box 548
Santa Cruz, NM 87567
Catalog $6. Lots of 12v stuff at good prices.

Real Goods Mail Order Trading Co.
555 Leslie St.
Ukiah, CA 95482-5507
(707) 468-9292
(800) 762-7325

Recreation Vehicle Products, Inc. (RVP)
P.O. Box 4020
Wichita, KS 67204
RV battery solar charger for Coleman air conditioners

Solar Electric Systems of Arizona
14415 N. 73rd Street
Scottsdale, AZ 85260
(602) 443-8520
(800) 999-8520
Will send periodic free *Solar Update* if you ask.

SOLAR AND 12-VOLT APPLIANCES

Solar Electric Specialties Co.

P.O. Box 537
Willits, CA 95490
(800) 344-2002
(solar and battery charging)

Sun Frost

Box 1101, Arcata
CA 95521
Expensive, but super-efficient refrigerator/freezers. Free info

Talmage Engineering

Box 497A, Beachwood Rd.
Kennebunkport, ME 04046
(207) 967-5945
$3 catalog has outstanding detail on specifications that makes it great for comparison shopping. Their prices are high.

Todd Engineering Sales

28706 Holiday Place
Elkhart, IN 46517
(Solar regulators)

MISCELLANEOUS PRODUCTS

Folding bicycle (Dahon)

833 Meridian St.
Duarte, CA 91010
(818) 305- 5264

Glo-Bar Assist Handle

Parts & Sales, Inc.
2101 Industrial Parkway
Elkhart, IN 46516
(800) 922-3410
(12-volt glowing handle)

Lil' Stanker Holding Tank Odor Fan

LSL Products
5807 Babcock, Ste 108
San Antonio, TX 78240
(210) 697-9502

Medical Equipment Co.

106 Quigley Blvd.
New Castle, DE 19720
(800) 322-3300
(All medical equipment)

Protect All, Inc.

1901 E. Via Burton St.
Anaheim, CA 92806
(800) 322-4491
(714) 635-4491
(total cleaning product)

RV Satellite Control

Townsend Systems
P.O. Box 424
Nottingham, NH 03290-0424
(800) 664-1679

TOW DOLLY

Automatic Equip Mfg.
  One Mill Road
  Industrial Park
  Pender, NE 68047
  (402) 385-3051

Classic Manufacturing Inc.
  21900 U.S. 12 W.
  Sturgis, MI 49091
  (616) 651-9319

Dethmers Mfg Co.
  P.O. Box 189
  Boyden, IA 51234
  (800) 543-3626
  (712) 725-2311

Master Tow Inc.
  Rte 6, Box 389
  Fayetteville, NC 28311
  (800) 522-2190

Remco
  P.O. Box 27998
  Omaha, NE 68127
  (800) 228-2481
  (402) 339-3398

Spearing Welding & Mfg.
  (Hitch-It)
  776 Newton Way
  Costa Mesa, CA 92627
  (800) 554-9956
  (714) 645-8583

TOWING EQUIPMENT

DrawTite Inc.
  40500 Van Born Rd.
  Canton, MI 48188
  (800) 521-0510
  (313) 722-7800

Eaz-Lift Hitches
  P.O. Box 489
  Sun Valley, CA 91353
  (818) 768-5880

Equal-i-zer (Lindon Hitch Inc.)
  475 N. State St.
  Lindon, UT 84042
  (801) 785-5181

Hensley Mfg. Co.
  1097 S. State Rd.
  Davison, MI 48423
  (800) 410-6580 (U.S.)
  (810) 658-0006 (Canada)

Pulliam Enterprises, Inc .
  (PullRite)
  1379 Jefferson Blvd.
  Mishawaka, IN 46545
  (800) 443-2307
  (219) 259-1520

Putnam Hitch Products Inc.
  P.O. Box 39
  Bronson, MI 49028-0039
  (800) 336-4271
  (517) 369-2165

Reese Hitch
  (Dual Cam Sway Control)
  P.O. Box 1706
  Elkhart, IN 46515
  (800) 326-0435
  (219) 264-7564

Remco
  4138 South 89th St
  P.O. Box 27998
  Omaha, NE 68127
  (800) 228-2481
  (402) 339-3398

Roadmaster, Inc.
  (StowMaster)
  5602 NE Skyport Way
  Portland, OR 97218
  (800) 669-9690
  (503) 288-9898

TRANSMISSION COOLER

Allison Transmissions
(Div. G.M. Corp.
P.O. Box 894
Indianapolis, IN 46206
(317) 242-0680

Carroll Supercharging Co. Inc.
14 Doty Rd.
Haskell, NJ 07420
(201) 835-1705

Cheshire Mfg. Co. Inc.
312 E. Johnson Ave.
Cheshire, CT 06410
(203) 272-3586

Coast Distribution System
P.O. Box 26888
San Jose, CA 95112
(408) 436-0877

Draw-Tite Consolidated
40500 Van Bom Rd.
Canton, MI 48188
(313) 722-7800

Hayden, Inc.
P.O. Box 848
Corona, CA 91718
(800) 854-4757
(714) 736-2665

P&E Industries Inc.
P.O. Box 810095
Boca Raton, FL 33481
(407) 241-6750

Perma-Cool
671 E. Edna Place
Covina, CA 91723
(818) 967-2777

Scotts Manufacturing Co.
28075 Ave. Stanford
Valencia, CA 91355
(800) 451-9461

Tekonsha Engineering Co.
537 N. Church St.
Tekonsha, MI 49092
(517) 767-4142

VINYL COVERS FOR RVS

Best RV
9335 Stevens Rd.
Santee, CA 92071
(800) 367-1791
(619) 448-7300

Gold Coast RV Products
3100 Wright Rd.
Camarillo, CA 93010
(800) 826-4467
(805) 981-7676

Dimensions in Business, Inc.
DIM*IT Suncreens
P.O. Box 147
Chappell Hill, TX 77426
(800) 873-4648

Kustom Fit Mfg Inc.
P.O. Box 218
Pioneer, OH 43554
(419) 737-2314

Sunguard Custom Covers
255 N. El Cielo Road
Palm Springs, CA 92262
(800) 334-5533
(619) 322-5533

Sunbuster
P.O. Box 637
Lincoln, MT 59639
(800) 543-5503

VENTS & VENT COVERS

Blacksmith Dist., Inc. (Vent)
P. O. Box 4405
Elkhart, IN 46514
(219) 262-3558

Fan-Tastic Vent Corp.
14720 Downer
Capac, MI 48014
(810) 742-0330

Kool-O-Matic Corp.
1831 Terminal Rd.
Niles, MI 49120

Maxx Air
5513 W. Sligh Ave.
Tampa, FL 33634
(800) 780-9893
(813) 872--9893

WATER FILTERS & PURIFIERS

Aqua-Flo Inc
6244 Frankford Ave
Baltimore, MD 21206
(410) 485-7600

Astro-Pure Inc.
3025 S.W. 2nd Ave.
Fort Lauderdale, FL 33315
(305) 971-9680

Bon Del Filters (Horner)
P.O. Box 213
Prescott, AZ 86302
(602) 964-8868

Campbell Manufacturing, Inc.
Spring & Railroad Streets
Bechtelsville, PA 19505
(800) 523-0224

DEL Industries
3428 Bullock Ln.
San Louis Obispo, CA 93401
(800) 676-1335

Distillerland Disc. Ctrs. Inc.
P.O. Box 21
Waterloo, IA 50704
(319) 235-7090

Equinox
% R. Harris
Box 17404
Boulder, CO 80308
(800) 765-7882
(303) 447-1172

Everpure Inc
660 N. Blackhawk Drive
Westmont, IL 60559
(919) 668-4007

MultiPure Drinking Systems
Box 590
Tempe, AZ 85280
(602) 820-7414

Western Purifier Co
P.O. Box 688
Woodland Hills, CA 91365
(818) 703-0444

Pure Water Enterprises, Inc
343 Broad Street
Lake Charles, LA 70601
(318) 439-4570

Water Quality Assn.
4151 Naperville Rd.
Lisle, IL 60532

The Watershed
National Testing Laboraties, Inc.
6555 Wilson Mills Rd.
Cleveland, OH 44143

WATER HEATERS

Atwood Mobile Products
  4750 Hiawatha Dr.
  Rockford, IL 61103
  (800) 847-7160

Chronomite Laboratories Inc.
  21011 S. Figueroa Street
  Carson, CA 90745
  (213) 320-9452
  (electric *instant* water heater)

Dometic Sales Corporation
  P. O. Box 490
  Elkhart, IN 46515
  (800) 544-4881

Evans Tempcon, Inc.
  701 Ann Street N.W.
  Grand Rapids, MI 49504
  (616) 361-2681

Mor-Flo Industries, Inc.
  P.O. Box 1956
  Santa Monica, CA 90404

Suburban Mfg Co, Inc.
  P.O. Box 399
  Dayton, TN 37321
  (615) 775-2131

WATER PUMPS/REGULATORS/TANKS

Best Plastics, Inc.
  19300 Grange St.
  Cassopolis, MI 46031
  (616) 641--5811
  (water holding tank).

LaVanture Products Co.
  P.O. Box 480
  Elkhart, IN 46515
  (800) 348-7625
  (water regulator)

ShurFlo Pump Mfg. Co
  12650 Westminster Ave.
  Santa Ana, CA 92706-2100
  (714) 554-7709
  (800) 854-3219

Triple Crown Products
  45-435 Van Buren St. #6
  Indio, CA 92201
  (619) 775-7585
  (water regulator)

WINDOWS/WINDSHIELDS

E-Z Windshield Repair
  P.O. Box 42351
  Kissimmee, FL 34742-3651
  (407) 933-7430

Glassparts RV Windshields, Inc.
  P.O. Box 30116
  Portland, OR 97230
  (503) 254-9694
  (repacements)

Peninsula Glass Co.
  6005 N.E. 21st Avenue
  Vancouver, WA 98682
  (800) 468-4323
  (206) 892-2029

Storm-Tite Inc.
  404 Egesz Street
  Winnipeg, MB
  Canada R2R 1XJ
  (204) 633-4808

Superglass Windshield Repair
  5 Benedict Road
  Buzzards Bay, MA 02532
  (508) 759-7799

Wildflower Enterprises, Inc.
  170 Topeka Street
  Branson, MO 65616
  (417) 338-2971

ALTERNATIVE ENERGY (SOLAR)

There are hundreds of publications on solar energy, but most do not apply to those who live and travel in RVs.

Better Use of... *by Michael Hackelman*
AATEC Publications
Box 7119
Ann Arbor, MI 48107
Somewhat dated as it does not describe newer solid-state electronics, but does include a wealth of info and tricks on using low-voltage electricity. $9.95 plus $1.50 postage.

(The) New Solar Electric Home by Joel Davidson
AATEC Publications   .
Box 7119
Ann Arbor, MI 48107.
The basic guide to photovoltaics. Updated version is more detailed than earlier book. $16.95 plus $1.50 postage.

Radio Shack Books:
> *Basic DC Circuits*
> *Getting Started in Electronics*
> *How to Use—your multimeter*

And other engineer notebooks
Accurate, easy to understand references for do-it-yourselfers.

Real Goods Alternative Energy Sourcebook
3041 Guidiville Road
Ukiah, CA 95482
(707) 468-9214
This $6.50 catalog is a textbook on solar energy, inverters, batteries and much more. Allows you to compare what's available.

RVers' Guide to Solar Battery Charging *by Noel and Barbara Kirkby.*
RV Solar Electric
14415 N. 73rd St.
Scottsdale, AZ 85260
(800) 999-8520
Contains lots more than just solar for the RV user. Has illustrated instructions on installation of solar panels. $14.45 ppd.

Buyers' Guides For RVs
(see also Directories and Magazines)

Hanley's Buyer's Guide to Van Conversions (1987)
Hanley's Publishing Company
482 North Milwaukee Avenue
Wheeling, IL 60090
Van conversion manufacturers with illustrations of products. Gives tips on van selection and review of chassis. $2.95.

How to Buy an RV Without Getting Ripped-off! *(see directories and guides)*

RV Standards & RV Buyers
Compiled by Recreational Vehicle Industry Association
P.O. Box 2999
Reston, VA 22090
(703) 620-6003
Requirements of Am. Nat'l Standard for installation of RV plumbing, heating, electrical systems. Send business size SASE for free copy.

(The) Green Book *by JD Gallant*
Quill Publishing
Box 490
Quilcene, WA 98376
Rates brands by quality and price. Essential resource for used RV.

Trailer Life Buyer's Guide
Trailer Life Enterprises, Inc.
P.O. Box 10241
Des Moines, IA 50381-0241
(800) 234-3450
Categorizes RVs by type with model, manufacturer, and size specifications. Updated annually. $4.95 plus $2 postage.

Woodall's RV Buyer's Guide
Woodall's Publishing Company
13975 W. Polo Trail Drive
Lake Forrest, IL 60045
(800) 323-9076
(708) 362-6700
Lists RVs by brand name, manufacturer, size, floor plans, standard and optional features and construction details for hundreds of models. Includes directory of RV dealers. Annual update $6.70 ppd.

CAMPING DIRECTORIES

American Automobile Association (AAA)

1000 AAA Dr.
Heathrow, FL 32746-5063
(407) 444-7962 or (913) 649-3213

Armed Forces FAM Camp Guide

U.S. Army AG Publications Center
2800 Eastern Blvd
Baltimore, MD 21220
Free guide lists services at FAM camps that are open to retired
military and DOD civilians who travel in RVs.

California Camping

Foghorn Press
212 Prentis Street
San Francisco, CA 94110

Camping in Queensland, Australia

Queensland National Parks
P.O. Box 155
North Quay, Queensland 4002 (Australia)

Camping in the National Park System

U.S. Government Printing Office #024-005-00846-2
Washington, DC 20402
Booklet: $3.50.

Directory For Traveling Elks West *by Carmichael Elks*

P.O. Box 765
Carmichael, CA 95609
Phone (916) 489-2103
For Elks only. Western states $8.50 ppd. Midwest: $8.50 ppd.

Disabled Driver's Mobility Guide *by Am. Automobile Assoc.*

1000 AAA Drive
Heathrow, FL 32746-5063
(913) 649-3213

Don Wright's Guide to Free Campgrounds

Cottage Publications
420 S. 4th St.
Elkhart, IN 46516
(219) 293-7553

CAMPING DIRECTORIES

Guide to National Parks in U.S.

U.S. Government Printing Office #024-005-0071-7
Washington, DC 20402
Booklet: $2.25.

How to Travel America Coast to Coast & Stay Free

 2420 N. Knoxville
Peoria, IL 61604-3645
(800) 475-0094
Price: $12.95 plus $3 shipping

KOA Directory/Road Atlas/Camping Guide

P.O. Box 30558,
Billings, MT 51994.
$2 by mail or free at any KOA campground.

Retired Military Almanac

P.O. Box 76, Depart. M
Washington, DC 20044
Gives the eligibility requirements and lists medical facilities and
family camping areas at military bases for retired military and their
dependents. Check for current price.

Trailer Life Campground/RV Park & Services Directory

P.O. Box 10241
Des Moines, IA 50381-0241
$15.95 ppd. Updated annually.

Wheelers RV Resort and Campground Guide

1310 Jarvis Avenue
Elk Grove Village, IL 60007
(800) 323-8899
(708) 981-0100
$14.95 plus $2.50 postage. Updated annually.

Woodalls North American Campground Directory

Woodall's Publishing Company
P.O. Box 5000
Lake Forrest, IL 60045
(800) 323-9076
(708) 362-6700
Price $19.95 plus $4 postage and handling.

Annual Directories often go up in price on reprints.

Publications

DIRECTORIES and GUIDES

See also Magazines and Newsletters

Americana Flea Market Guide

P.O. Box 702, Palmyra, NJ 08065
Complete guide. Forward gives history of flea markets.
$10.95 plus $2 shipping

Backwoods Solar Electric Systems

8530 Rapid Lightning Creek, Sandpoint, ID 83864
(208) 263-4290
Catalog and Planning Guide $4. Free quarterly newsletter.

Battery Service Manual

The Battery Council International
111 East Wacker, Chicago, IL 60601

Bus Conversions

4517 La Vante, Long Beach, CA 90815
(310) 432-7645

Chevrolet Trailering Guide

Chevrolet Motor Division, Special Vehicles Dept.
30007 Van Dyke Ave., Room 246-06
Warren, MI 48094

Chrysler Towing Information

Chrysler Corp.
P.O. Box 1718, Detroit, MI 48288

Clark's Flea Market, U.S.A.

419 Garcon Point Rd.,Milton, FL 32583
Comprehensive guide covering flea markets and swap meets in all of
the states. $7.50 by mail includes tax

Digest of Motor Laws *(by AAA)*

1000 AAA Dr., Heathrow, FL 32746-5063
(913) 649-3213
(State by state listing of vehicle registration and licensing laws)

Directory of Free Vacation & Travel Information *edited by Raymond Carlson*

Pilot Industries, Inc.
103 Cooper Street, Babylon, New York 11702

DIRECTORIES and GUIDES

(The) Directory of North American Fairs, Festivals and Expositions
Amusement Business
P.O. Box 5022, Brentwood, TN 37024-9776

Directory Of Theme & Amusement Parks *edited by Raymond Carlson and Eleanor Popelka.* Published 1988
Pilot Books,
103 Cooper Street, Babylon, NY 11702

Dollars In Your Driveway
Halo House Publisher
617 Westland Drive , Greensburg, PA 15601

Europe Free! the RV Travel Guide 1987 *by David Shore*
1437 Lucile , Los Angeles, CA 90026
Tips on campgrounds, language, shopping, , money etc. $5.95.

Festivals (by region)
Landau Communications
1032 Irving St. Ste. 604, San Francisco, CA 94122
Send for price list

Ford's RV & Trailer Towing Guide
Ford Motor, Ford Division
300 Ren Center, P.O. Box 43306, Detroit, MI 48243

GMC Recreational & Trailer Guide
Customer Service Department
31 Judson Street, Pontiac, MI 48058

Going Places: (The) Guide to Travel Guides *by Greg Hayes & Joan Wright*
Harvard Common Press
535 Albany St., Boston, MA 02118
(617) 423-5803
Travel books, magazines, newsletters around the world

(The) Green Book *by JD Gallant*
Quill Publishing
Box 490, Quilcene, WA 98376
(360) 765-3846
Rates various RV brands for quality and price.

DIRECTORIES and GUIDES

Greener Pastures Relocation Guide *by Alfred Shattuck*

Prentice Hall, Inc.
Sylvan Ave, Englewood Cliffs, NJ 07632
(201) 592-2000 or (800) 223-1360

Guide to Free Attractions *by Don & Pam Wright*

Cottage Publications, Inc.
420 S. 4th St., Elkhart, IN 46516
(219) 293-7553
State listings of free tourist attractions. $14.95 plus $1.50 P&H.

Guide Book To Free Industry Tours *by Wade Chapman*.

Kaywaden Associates
P. 0. Box 371, Hinsdale, IL 60521
(72 pages $5)
Lists companies that offer free tours. Covers 27 industries in 36 states.

How to Buy an RV Without Getting Ripped-off!

by JD Gallant
Quill Publishing
Box 490, Quilcene, WA 98376

How to Travel America Coast to Coast and Stay Free

RV Guide— 2420 N. Knoxville, Peoria, IL 61604-3645
(800) 475-0094
Price $12.95 plus $3 shipping & handling

ICA (Inn Care of America)

P.O. Box 1204, Clarksville, TN 37041
(800) 489-6277
Family Physicians service for travelers. Medical Assist Passport Plan.
$24.95—$39.95.

Kelley Blue Book Official Motorhome Guide
Kelley Blue Book Official Travel Trailer Guide

5 Oldfield
PO Box 19691, Irvine, CA 92713-9981
(800-444-1743
Price $47 for each of the above books.

DIRECTORIES and GUIDES

Living on 12 Volts with Ample Power by *Davis Smead and Ruth Ishihara*

Ample Power Co.
2442 NW Market St. #43, Seattle, WA 98107
(800) 541-7789 or (206) 789-1138

Living On Wheels: The Complete Guide to Motorhomes *by John Boardman*

Tab Books, Inc.
Blue Ridge Summit, PA 17214.
Technical book containing much helpful information on maintenance and operation of a motor home. $12.95

(The) Magnificent Peninsula *by Jack Williams*

P.O. Box 203,Sausalito, CA 94966
(415) 332-8635
Mexico's Baja, California. $17.95 plus $3 shipping.

Military RV Camping & Rec Areas Around The World

Military Living Publications
P.O. Box 2347, Falls Church, VA 22042
More than 225 listings worldwide. Includes facilities, prices, reservations, regional maps, and eligibility information.

Motorhome & Truck Camper Trade-in Guide & Camping and Travel Trailer Trade-in Guide

Book Division, Intertec Publishing Corp.
PO Box 12901, Overland Park, Kansas 66212-9981

N.A.D.A. RV Appraisal Guide

P. O. Box 7800, Costa Mesa, CA 92628
(714) 556-8511
(800) 966-6232 or (800) 544-6232 for corporate office
Call for current price. Used RV value guides.

NCOA Publications

409 Third St. SW, Suite 200, Washington, DC 20024
(800) 867-2755
Many publications on aging, care giving, etc. Send for list.

DIRECTORIES and GUIDES

National Directory Of Free Tourist Attractions
edited by Raymond Carlson and Maria Maiorino.
Pilot Books
103 Cooper Street, Babylon, NY 11702
Lists over 1150 freebies. Check for current price.

National Parks Trade Journal
Taverly-Churchill Publishing Co.
Wawona Station.Yosemite National Park, CA 95389

Peggy's SwapMeet & FleaMarket Guide
P.O. Box 393, Hicksville, NY 11802-0393
Includes a section listing arts and craft shows, steet fairs, antique
shows and festivals. By mail, price is $8.50

(The) Professional Driver's Truck Stop Locator
P.O. Box 1385, Palatine, IL 60078-1385
Gives over 2100 locations. Check for current price. Sold at many
truck stops.

Solar Living Source Book
Real Goods Trading Corp.
555 Leslie Street, Ukiah, CA 95482-5507
(800) 762-7325 or (707) 468-9292
 Catalog with comparison of products and prices. $23

Rest Area Guide to U.S. and Canada
6965 El Camino Real, 105-406, Carlsbad, CA 92009
(619) 438-0514
Price $12.95 plus $2 shipping and handling

Retirement Choices for the Time of Your Life and
RV Travel in Mexico *by John Howells* and
Choose Mexico *by John Howells and Donald Menvin.*
Gateway Books
1750 Post Street, Suite 111, San Francisco, CA 94115
Order from, or purchase at, local bookstores.

(The) Road Ahead: A Stroke Recovery Guide
1420 Ogden Street, Denver, CO 80218
Advice to both victims and caregivers. $14.50.

DIRECTORIES and GUIDES

RV Buyers Guide
2575 Vista Del Mar Drive, Ventura, CA 93001
(800) 541-1010 or (800) 234-3450

RV Owners Operation & Maintenance Manual
Intertec Pub. Corp, Technical Pub. Division
P.O. Box 12901, Overland Park, KS 66212

RV Service Guide
760 Auburn Avenue, Buffalo, NY 14222
For motor coach owners. LP gas outlets & diesel repair shops.

RVers' Guide by *Noel and Barbara Kirkby*
RV Solar Electric
14415 N. 73rd St., Scottsdale, AZ 85260
(800) 999-8520
 (602) 443-8520

(The) Senior Citizens' Survival Manual by *Bill Kaysing*
Bellwether Press
321 Hampton Drive,Venice, CA 90291
Health, living well, and getting more out of your retirement.

Shop Manuals by Helm, Inc.
(800) 782-4356 Call for list of what is available.

RX for RV Performance and Mileage by *Geraghty and Estes*
Trailer Life Publications
2575 Vista Del Mar Drive, Ventura, CA 93001
(800) 234-3450 to order by credit card

RV Repair and Maintenance Manual by *Livingston*
Trailer Life Publications
2575 Vista Del Mar Dr., Ventura, CA 93001
(800) 234-3450 to order by credit card.

The RV Handbook by *Bill Estes*
Trailer Life Publications
2575 Vista Del Mar Drive, Ventura, CA 93001
(800) 234-3450 to order by credit card.

Special Events Directory
P.O. Box 702, Palmyra, NJ 08065
All-inclusive annual directory. Includes all trade shows. $75.

DIRECTORIES and GUIDES

Steam and Gas Show Directory

Stemgas Publishing Co.
P.O. Box 328, Lancaster, PA 17068
Lists agricultural/mechanical related events throuout U.S.A. Focus is
on antique tractors and steam engines. Includes list of shows. $6 ppd.

The Trucker's Friend: Diesel Fuel Directory

P.O. Box 476, Clearwater, FL 34617
(800) 338-6317 or (813) 446-2866
Over 4,000 locations with their facilities. $11.95 ppd.

The 12 Volt Doctor's Practicle Handbook for the RV and Motorhome *by Edgar Beyn*

BeeLine   or   E. Beyn, SPA Creek Instruments
P.O. Box 748   616 3rd St.
Hobe Sound, FL 33475   Annapolis, MD 21403
(301) 267-6565
Explains how electrical systems work

Union 76 Disposal Stations Directory

Union Oil Company of California
Box 7600, Los Angeles, CA 90051
(Free for the asking)

Wiring 12 Volts for Ample Power *by David Smead and Ruth Ishihara*

Ample Power Co., 1150 NW 52nd St., Seattle, WA 98107
(800) 541-7789

Woodall's RV How-To Guide/RV Owners Handbook

Dept 2054, P.O. Box 5000, Lake Forrest, IL 60045-5000
(800) 323-9076
Customizing and repairing all types of RVs. $6.95 ppd.

EARNING MONEY on the ROAD
Also see Directories and guides and magazines and newsletters

Americana Flea Market
P.O. Box 702
Palmyra, NJ 08065

Antique Gazette
6949 Charlotte Pike #106
Nashville, TN 37209
(800) 660-6143
(615) 352-0941

(The) Career Press
P.O. Box 34
Hawthorne, NJ 07507
(800) CAREER-1 (U.S. only)
(201) 427-2037
Write or call for free catalog.

New Careers Center, Inc.
P.O. Box 339-CT
Boulder, CO 80306
(303) 447-1087
Write or call for list of titles.

Clark's Flea Market, U.S.A.
419 Garcon Point Rd.
Milton, FL 32583

HT (healthcare travelers)
P.O. Box 48
Eden, MD 21822-9900
(800) 948-8728
For traveling health care
professonals.

Show Biz Directory
P.O. Box 12811
Salem, OR 97309
(800) 873-1840
(503-371-3627

Summer Jobs
Peterson's Guides,
Princeton, NJ 08540

Sunshine Artist
1736 North Highway 427
Longwood, FL 32750-3410
(800) 597-2573

The following books are available at bookstores or from:
Writer's Digest Books, 1507 Dana Ave, Cincinnati, OH 45207

Artists Market
Lists places where you can sell your work.

How You Can Make $25,000 a Year Writing
 Explains how to be a freelance writer.

National Directory of Shops/galleries/Shows/Fair
Lists of art and craft fairs. $14.45.

Photographer's Market
Lists places to sell photos.

Song Writer's Market
Where to market your songs and avoid song sharks.

Writer's Market
Places to sell your writing. Updated annually.

BOOKS ON THE RV LIFESTYLE

An Alternative Lifestyle by Ron & Barb Hofmeister
R&B Publications
101 Rainbow Drive #2179
Livingston, TX 77351
Economic and social aspects of full-time RVing. $12.95

Exploring Europe by RV by Dennis & Tina Jaffe
The Globe Pequot Press
P.O. Box 833
Old Saybrook, CT 06475
Best ways to buy, lease, rent, or exchange an RV. $14.95

Full-Time RVing: Complete Guide to Life on Open Road
by Bill and Jan Moeller

TL Enterprises, Inc.
2575 Vista Del Mar Drive
Ventura, CA 93001
$14.95 plus $2 postage.

Home Is Where You Park It *by Kay Peterson*
RoVers Publications
100 Rainbow Drive
Livingston, TX 77351
(800) 9-ROVERS
Deals with all aspects of living on the road. Blend of practical and
psychological aspects makes this how-to book easy to read. $9.95.

Living In A Motor Home *by Laura Wolfe*
Woodsong Graphics, Inc.
P.O. Box 238
New Hope, PA 18938
Author shares RVing experiences. $6.95 ppd.

(The) RV Handbook *by Bill Estes*
Trailer Life Books
2575 Vista Del Mar Drive
Ventura, CA 93001
(800) 234-3450
RV systems, maintenance, and equipment $29.95

BOOKS ON THE RV LIFESTYLE

RV Owners Operation & Maintenance Manual

Intertec Publishing Corporation
P.O. Box 12901
Overland Park, KS 66212
Explains electrical, LP-gas, & water systems. Write for current price.

RVing From A To Z *by Bill Farlow*

Cottage Publications
420 S. 4th St.
Elkhart, IN 46516
(219) 293-7553

Survival Of The RV Snowbirds *by Joe & Kay Peterson*

RoVers Publications
100 Rainbow Drive
Livingston, TX 77351
(800) 976-8377
How to save money by using RV self-containment. $9.95 ppd.

Travel Europe With Your Motor Home
by Nancy & Ralph Rosenlund

Bristol Publishing Co.
P.O. Box 81
Bristol, IN 46507
For independent travelers who enjoy the back roads.

Two sources for purchasing books on RVing

Cottage Publications	**Workamper Book Store**
420 S. 4th St.	201 Hiram Rd.
Elkhart, IN 46516	Heber Springs, AR 72543
(219) 293-7553	(800) 446-5627
	(501) 362-2637

MAGAZINES & NEWSLETTERS

Accent On Living
Cheever Publications
P.O. Box 700
Bloomington, IL 61702
(309) 378-2961
(Geared to handicapped people)

Bus Conversion Magazine
4517 LaVante St.
Long Beach, CA 90813
(310) 432-7645

Camping Canada Magazine
2585 Skymark Ave. #306
Mississauga, ON CN L4W 4L5
(905) 624-8218
RV Consumer and RV Trade mag.

Disabled Outdoors
5223 South Lorel Ave
Chicago, IL 60638
(218) 387-9100

Escapees Magazine
100 Rainbow Drive
Livingston, TX 77351
(800) 976--8377
(for serious RVers)

Family Motor Coaching
8291 Clough Pike
Cincinnati, OH 45244-9928
(513) 474-3622
(800) 543-3622
Price includes all club benefits.

4WD and Off Road
6420 Wilshire Blvd.
Los Angeles, CA 90048
(213) 782-2360

Hi-Way Herald
P.O. Box 1109
Des Moines, IA 50380-1097
(800) 234-3450

Home Power Magazine
Box 520
Ashland, OR 97520
(800) 707-6585
Living on 12 Volts $22.50/yr.

M & S Technical Serv.
74A Bell St.
West Babylon, NY 11704
(516) 726-2045
Newsletter on Ford diesels

Military Living
R & R Report
P.O. Box 2347
Falls Church, VA 22042
(703) 237-0203

Monitoring Times
(Short wave radio frequencies)
Box 98
Brasstown, NC 28902

Motor Home
P.O. Box 54461
Boulder, CO 80322-4461
(800) 678-1201

Movin' On
R & B Publications
101 Rainbow Drive #2179
Livingston, TX 77351-9300
$1.50/issue

National Bus Trader
9698 West Judson Road
Polo, IL 61064
(815) 946-2341

Northeast Outdoors
70 Edwin Ave, Box 2180
Waterbury, CT 06722
(203) 755-0158

MAGAZINES & NEWSLETTERS

Nuts & Boltz
P. O. Box 123
Butler MD 21023-0123
(410) 584-7574
(800) 888-0091
Consumer newsletter.
$19.95/yr 12 issues

Project Vote Smart
129 NW Fourth St. #204
Corvallis, OR 97330
(503) 754-2746
(800) 622-SMART

PV Network News
2303 Cedros Circle
Santa Fe, NM 87505
(505) 473-1067
Quarterly: solar usage $15/yr.

Rolling Ventures
P.O. Box 2190-1941
Pahrump, NV 89041-2190

RV Business
P.O. Box 1109
Des Moines, IA 50380-1097
(800) 234-3450

RV Journal
P.O. Box 7675
Laguna Niguel, CA 92607
(714) 489-7729
Quarterly: Southern California

RV Times
P.O. Box 160, 129 W. 2nd Ave.
Qualicum Beach BC V9K 1S7
Canada
(604) 752-8266

RV Trade Digest
Continental Pub.
P.O. Box 1805
Elkhart, IN 46515
(800) 380-2345
(219) 295-1962

Solar Update
14415 N. 73rd Street
Scottsdale, AZ 85260
(800) 999-8520
Newsletter $2

Tightward Gazette
RR#1 Box 3570
Leeds, ME 04263

Trailer Life
3601 Calle Tecate
Camarillo, CA 93012
(805) 667-4100

Treasure Hunters
Fisher Research Lab.
200 W. Wilemott Road
Los Banos, CA 93635

Woodall's RV Traveler
P.O. Box 247
Greenville, MI 48838
(616) 754-2251
($12 year)

Workamper News
201 Hiram Road
Heber Springs, AR 72543
(800) 446-5627
(501) 362-2637

Workers On Wheels
101 Rainbow Dr. #2174
Livingston, TX 77351
(409) 327-0079 Code 2174

FOR THE HANDICAPPED

(Also see Health Organizations and Support Groups)

Accent On Information

P.O. Box 700
Bloomington, IL 61701
(309) 378-2961
Information concerning handicapped persons. Publishes: "Accent On Living" quarterly.

Mobility International

Colombo Street
London SE1 8DP, England
Provides information on international contacts and travel facilities for the handicapped.

Society for Advancement of Travel for the Handicapped

1012 14th Street Northwest, Suite 803
Washington, DC 20005
Acts as information clearinghouse and referral service for travel and tourism opportunities for the handicapped, senior citizens, and the mentally retarded.

Tennessee's Silent Campers: (Deaf campers.)

Lloyd Billingsley, Club secretary
3331 Percy Presit Drive
Nashville, TN 37214
Operates as chapter of National Campers & Hikers Assn.

SINGLE PEOPLE

Many RV clubs also have chapters for single travelers.

Fifty Upward Network (FUN)

P.O. Box 4714
Cleveland, OH 44126
Forsingle, middle-aged *women*. Seminars/ bimonthly newsletter.

Loners of America, Inc.

Route 2, Box 85E
Elsinore, MO 63937

Loners on Wheels, Inc.

P.O. Box 1355
Poplar Bluff, MO 63901
(314) 785-2420
Singles only. Monthly newsletter. Rallies and caravaning.

Partners in Travel

P.O. Box 491145
Lo Angeles, CA 90049
For those seeking travel companions.

RVing Women

P.O. Box 1940 Dept. C
Apache Junction, AZ 85219
(602) 983-4678
Support network for single women RVers. $39/yr. (Outside U.S. $45)

Travel Companion Exchange

Box 833
Amityville, NY 11701.
Fee ranges from $5 to $11 a month. Write for information.

Travel Partners Club

Box 2368,
Crystal River, FL 32629
Most members are widowed. Bimonthly newsletter.

Wandering Individuals' Network (WIN)

% Dorothy Prince, P.O. Box 2010
Sparks, NV 89432-2010
Social club for *single* RV owners born after 1926. Newsletter, rallies.
Puts out newsletter and holds many rallies.

RV CLUBS

Avion Travelcade Club

1300 East Empire Avenue
Benton Harbor, MI 49022
Restricted to owners of Avion trailers.

(Baby) Boomers

%Harold & Gloria Michelson
101 Rainbow Dr., Apt. #2630
Livingston, TX 77351-9300
For those born around 1940-60 era. Newsletter $20/yr. Canada $35

Canadian Family Camping Federation

P.O. Box 397
Rexdale, Ontario, Canada M9W 1R3

Christian Motor Coach Association

P.O. Box 2686
Roswell, NM 88202-2686
Non-denominational for traveling Christians.

CMCA (Australia Caravan Club)

% Secretary
P.O. Box 327
Cardiff, NSW 2285 (Australia)
(Publishes The Wanderer)

Escapees, Inc.

100 Rainbow Drive
Livingston, TX 77351
(800) 976-8377
(409) 327-8873
Support network for those who live and travel in an RV. Dues: $50/yr.
plus a one-time $10 registration fee.

Family Campers & RVers Association

(Formerly Natioanl Campers & Hikers Assoc. NCHA)

4804 Transit Road	*In Canada:*
Building 2	51 West 22nd Street
Depew, NY 14043-4704	Hamilton, Ontario L9C 4N5

(716) 668-6242 Publishes "Camping News"

RV CLUBS

Family Motor Coach Association (FMCA)
8291 Clough Pike
Cincinnati, OH 45244-9928
(513) 474-3622
(800) 543-3622
Restricted to motor home users. Dues $35.

Fifth Wheel Owners Club
1621 Park View Pl.
Edmond, OK 73003

Foremost Motorcade Club
1221 NW Stallings Drive
Nacogdoches, TX 75961
Foremost owners only.

Friendly Roamers
Bob & Joyce Keagle
P.O. Box 527
Waldport, OR 97394
Membership open to singles and couples.

Gay & Lesbian RVers
RV Adventuring
708 Gravenstein Hwy North #164
Sebastopol, CA 95472
(707) 892-9023

Good Sam Club
P.O. Box 11079
Des Moines, IA 50380-1097
Phone: (800) 234-3450

Happy Wheelers International
P.O. Box 503
Mishawaka, Indiana 46544

Holiday Rambler RV Club
600 E. Wabash, P.O. Box 587
Wakarusa, IN 46573
(219) 862-7330.

RV CLUBS

International Caravanning Association (ICA)
U.S. Contact: Wayne Kispert
4042 Golfside Dr.
 Orlando, FL 32808
(206) 459-4316
Canadian Contact: Ivan Fox (416) 634-4003

International Family Recreation Association
P.O. Box 520
 Gonzales, FL 32560-0520
(904) 477-7992 or 479-8393

Laborers For Christ *(volunteers)*
The Lutheran Church-Missouri Synod
1333 South Kirkwood Road
St. Louis, MO 63122-7295

Loners of America, Inc.
Route 2, Box 85E
Elsinore, MO 63937
Member-owned-and-operated singles RV club.

Loners on Wheels, Inc.
P.O. Box 1355
Poplar Bluff, MO 63901
(314) 785-2420
Singles only. Monthly newsletter. Rallies and caravaning.

(The) Motorhome Travelers Association, Inc.
P.O. Box 7505
Pensacola, FL 32514
(904) 474-1830 For motor home owners only.

National Association of Trailer Owners (NATO)
Box 1418, 2105 Tuttle
Sarasota, FL 33578
(800) 237-NATO
For owners of all RVs. Mail service for members.

RV CLUBS

National Camping Association
353 West 56th Stret
New York, NY 10019

National RV Owners Club
P.O. Drawer 17148
Pensacola, FL 32522-8393
(904) 477-7992
Publishes *The Recreation Advisor.*

New Zealand Motor Caravan Assn. Inc. (N.Z.M.C.A.)
P.O. Box 107
Moerewa, Bay of Islands (New Zealand)

Recreational Vehicle Industry Association (RVIA)
P.O. Box 2999, 1896 Preston White Drive
Reston, VA 22090
(703) 620-6003
(800) 336-0154

RV Consumer Group
P.O. Box 520
Quilcene, WA 98376
(360) 765-3846
Help line, price and rating reports.

RVing Women
P.O. Box 1940
Apache Junction, AZ 85217
(602) 983-4678
Support network for women RVers. Newsletter and directory.

Servants On Wheels Ever Ready (SOWERS)
P.O. Box 175
Ten Mile, TN 377880
(615) 334-3435
Christian volunteers to help on construction in exchange for parking.

Special Military Active /Retired Travel Club (S.M.A.R.T)
600 University Office Blvd. Ste. 1-A
Pensacola, FL 32504
Promote comradeship. Holds semiannual musters.

RV CLUBS

(U.S.) Submarine Veteran RV'rs

% Lorie Sullivan
922 Elizabeth St.
Pueblo, CO 81003.
For RVers who have served with the U.S. submarine force.

Wally Byam Caravan Club, International (WBCCI)

P.O. Box 612
Jackson Center, OH 45334
(513) 596-5211
For Airsteam owners.

WBCCI Full Timers Club

Contact Terry Tyler
4 Columbia Drive
E. Greenbush, NY 12061
Publishes "Down The Road" newsletter.

Wandering Individuals' Network (WIN)

% Dorothy Prince
P.O. Box 2010
Sparks, NV 89432-2010
Social club for *single* RV owners born after 1926.
Puts out newsletter and holds many rallies.

RVJ Reservation Service
P.O. Box 7675
Laguna Niguel, CA 92607
(800) 445-4334
Handles all county and state campground reservations
for clubs and organizations in California.

SPECIAL INTEREST

American Youth Hostels (AYH)
P.O. Box 37613
Washington, DC 20013-7613
(800) 444-6111
(202) 783-6161
Affiliated with Intl.Youth Hostel Assn. in 70 nations.

Clowns of America, International, Inc.
% David Barnett
Box 570
Lake Jackson, TX 77566
(409) 297-6699
Clowns, magicians, puppeteers, jugglers. Monthly pub.

Country Music Association, Inc. (CMA)
1 Music Circle South
Nashville, TN 37203
(800) 998-4636
(615) 244-2840
Promotes country music throughout world.

Coupon Exchange Club
P.O. Box 13708
Wauwatosa, WI 53213
Buys and sells coupons from individuals and charitable organizations.

Family History Library
35 NW Temple
Salt Lake City, UT 84150
(801) 240-2331
Training activities and client search. Publishes books, work forms, etc.

Creative Clown Company
New Haven, CT 06511
(203) 877-3869
Information on clowning or to hire a professional clown.

Golf Card, International
P.O. Box 7021
Englewood, CO 80155
(800) 453-4260
or call (800) 522-9232 in Tallahassee, Florida

SPECIAL INTEREST

League of American Bicyclists
190 W. Ostend St., Suite 120
Baltimore, MD 21230-3755
(410) 539-3399
National organization of bicyclists. Info on bike tours.

National Assoc. Retired Federal Employees (NARFE)
1533 New Hampshire Ave. N.W.
Washington DC 20036-1279
(800) 456-8410
(202) 234-0832

National Audubon Society
950 3rd Avenue
New York, NY 10022

National League of American Pen Women, Inc.
1300 17th Street Northwest
Washington DC 20036
(202) 785-1997
Workshops and contests in writing and music composition.

National Speakers Association
3877 North 7th St., Ste 350
Phoenix, AZ 85014
(602) 265-7403

National Wildlife Federation
1412 -16th St., NW
Washington, D.C. 20036

National Woodcarvers Association
7424 Miami Avenue
Cincinnati, OH 45243
(513) 561-9051
or (513) 561-9051
Membership dues $11 includes subscription to *Chip Chats* magazine.

National Writers Club
1450 South Havana
Aurora, CO 80012
(303) 751-7844
Helps freelance writers. Publishes monthly newsletter.

SPECIAL INTEREST

Optimist International

4494 Lindell Blvd.
St. Louis, MO 63108
(314) 371-6000

Professional Photographers of America

57 Forsyth St. NW, Suite 1600
Atlanta, GA 30303
(800) 742-7468
(404) 522-8600
Maintain standards and expand market for photography. Newsletter.

Sierra Club

530 Bush Street
San Francisco, CA 94108

Toastmasters International

P.O. Box 9052
Mission Viejo, CA 92690
(714) 858-8255

United States Chess Federation

186 Route 9W
New Windsor, NY 12553
(800) 388-5464
(914) 562-8350
Fax 914-561-2437

HEALTH and MEDICAL

Agency for Health Care Policy and Research AHCPR
2101 East Jefferson St., Suite 501
Rockville, MD 20852
(800) 358-9295 or (301) 594-1364
Provides documents free through publications clearinghouse.

Aides (HIV) (and other sexually transmitted diseases)
215 Park Ave. South, Suite 714
New York, NY 10003
(800) 342-2437 or (800) 227-8922
Open 24 hours a day. Refers you to local help, physicians, etc.

Alzheimer's Association
919 North Michican Ave., Suite 1000
Chicago, IL 60611
(800) 272-3900
(800) 438-4380
Information and supportive help. Publishes *The 36-Hour Day.*

American Association of Homes for the Aging
901 E. St. NW, Suite 500
Washington, DC 20004-2837
(202) 783-2242

American Cancer Society, Inc
1599 Clifton Rd. N.E.
Atlanta, GA 30329-4251
(404) 320-3333
(212) 371-2900
Services: Offers information, counseling, and transportation.

American Diabetes Association, Inc
Texas affiliate: 9430 Research Blvd. Bld 2, Suite 300
Austin, TX 78759
(800) 868-7888
Services: Patient and public education and assistance.

American Foundation For the Blind
11 Ten Plaza, Suite 300
New York, NY 10001
(212) 502-7600
Has directories of agencies serving visually impaired. Quarterly pub.

HEALTH and MEDICAL

American Heart Association

7272 Greenville Avenue   or   2425 W. Loop South 330
Dallas, TX 75231   Houston, TX 77027
(800) 586-4872
(214) 373-6300

American Lung Association

1740 Broadway
New York NY 10019
(800) 586-4872
(212) 315-8700
Promotes anti-smoking, anti-pollution education.

American Occupational Therapy Assoc.

P.O. Box 1725
1383 Piccard Dr.
Rockville, MD 20849-1725
(301) 948-9626

Arthritis Foundation

1314 Spring Street Northwest
Atlanta, GA 30309-2898
(800) 464-6240
(404) 872-7100   Provides information.

Arthritis Society (Canada)

250 Bloor St. East, Suite 901
Toronto, Canada M4W 3P2
(416) 967-1414
Gives info about cause, cure, and prevention of arthritis.

Canadian Heart Association

Suite 1200, 1 Nicholas Street
Ottawa, Ontario, Canada K1N 7B7
Services: Research and education related to heart disease.

Cerebral Palsy Association

106 E. 31st Terrace
Kansas City, MO 64111
(816) 531-4189
(800) 325-8173
Offers aid and information.

HEALTH and MEDICAL

Children of Aging Parents (CAPS)
1609 Woodbourne Rd. Suite 302A
Levittown, PA 19057
(215) 945-6900

Cystic Fibrosis Foundation
2250 North Druid Hills Road
Atlanta, GA 30326
(404) 325-6793

Diabetes Association
9201 Ward Parkway, Suite 300
Kansas City, MO 64114
(816) 361-3361

Dogs for the Deaf
10175 Wheeler Road
Central Point, OR 97502
(503) 826-9200

Emphysema *call (800) 322-3300*

Guiding Eyes for the blind
611 Granite Springs Road
Yorktown Heights, NY 10598
(800) 942-0149
(914) 245-4024

Hospice Supplies Store
200 State Road
S. Deerfield, MA 01373
(800) 646-6460

Leukemia Society of America, Inc.
600 Third Avenue
New York, NY 10016
(212) 473-8484

The Living Bank (Organ Donors)
P.O. Box 6725
Houston, TX 77265
(800) 528-2971—24 hours a day.
Maintains national registry for organ and tissue donors.

HEALTH and MEDICAL

Medic Alert Foundation

P.O. Box 1009
Turlock, CA 95381-1009
(800) 344-3226
(209) 668-3333
Lifetime membership $15 gives you a wallet-size condensation of medical history with bracelet or necklace marked "Alert."

Medical Management & Equipment Co.

106 Quigley Blvd.
New Castle, DE 19720
(800) 322-3300
Sends out information on all diseases and carries medical equipment.

MedReport Corporation

7 South Main St., Ste. 201
P.O. Box 271780
West Hartford, CT 06107-1780
(800) 236-4915, Dept. 107
(860) 231-2408
Your medical information immediately sent to doctors and hospitals by voice, fax, or modem.

National Association for Home Care

519 C St. NE
Stanton Park
Washington, DC 20002
(202) 547-7424

National Association of the Deaf

814 Thayer Avenue
Silver Spring, MD 20910-4505
(301) 587-1788.

National Association on Drug Abuse Problems

355 Lexington Avenue
New York. NY 10017-6601
(212) 986-1170
Services include ducation and referral.

HEALTH and MEDICAL

National Cancer Institute

Building 31, Room 10A30
9000 Rockville Pike
Bethesda, MD 30014
(800) 4-CANCER

National Council On Aging (NCOA)

Dept. 5087
Washington, DC 20061-5087
(202) 424-1200
Information and resources. Publishes literature.

National Hearing Aid Society

20361 Middlebelt Road
Livonia, MI 48152
(313) 478-2610
Improves standards of hearing aids and education.

National Hospice Organization

1901 N. Moore St., Ste 901
Arlington, VA 22209
(703) 243-5900

National Kidney Foundation

30 East 33rd St.
New York, NY 10016.
Offers information on prevention, treatment, and cure.

National Mental Health Consumer Clearinghouse

1211 Chestnut St.
Philadelphia, PA 19107
(800) 553-4539

National Multiple Sclerosis Society

733 Third Avenue
New York, NY 10017-5706
(212) 986-3240

National Parkinson Foundation

1501 NW 9th Ave.
Miami, FL 33136
(800) 327-4545

HEALTH and MEDICAL

National Stroke Association

8480 East Orchard Road, Suite 1000
Englewood, CO 80111
(800) STROKES
(303) 771-1700

National Technical Information Service

5285 Port Royal Road
Springfield, VA 22161
(703) 487-4650

Organ Donors/Transplants

P.O. Box 13770
Richmond, VA 23225
(800)-24 DONOR (for voice information)
(804) 330-8602 (for answers to questions)

Parkinson's Disease Foundation

650 W. 168th St.
New York, NY 10032
(800) 457-6676

Prevent Blindness America

500 E. Remington Road
Schaumburg, IL 60173
(800) 331-2020

Public Health Service

U.S. Dept. of Health and Human Services
Executive Office Center, Suite 501
2101 East Jefferson St.
Rockville, MD 20852

MedReport Corporation

7 South Main Street, Suite 201
P.O. Box 271780
West Hartford, CT 06107-1780
(860) 231-2408

Sky-Med (Emergency Transport Services)

4422 Civic Center Plaza, Ste. 101
Scottsdale, AZ 85251
(800) 475-9633 or (602) 946-5188

SERVICE and INFORMATION

American Association of Retired Persons (AARP)

1909 "K" Street Northwest
Washington, DC 20049
(202) 872-4700
Legislation, community service, and information.

American Chamber of Commerce

4232 King St.
Alexandria, VA 22302
(800) 394-2223
(703) 998-0072)

American Red Cross

430 17th St. Northwest
Washington, DC 20006-0000
(800) 272-0024 (blood)
(800) 654-1247 (bone marrow)
(800) 842-2200 (disaster relief)
(202) 737-8300
Blood and disaster services. Publishes first aid and safety books.

Bankcard Holders of America

Box 524, Branch Dr.
Salem, VA 24153
(800) 638-6407
(540) 389-5445
Fights for rights of credit card users. Sells list of banks that do not charge annual fee or have reduced interest rates ($1.50 per list.)

Corp. for National Services

1201 New York Ave. NW
Washington DC 20525
(202) 606-5000
Federal agency for all volunteer services.

Customs information *see U.S. Customs Service*

Department of Education

Special Education and Rehab Services
330 C St. SW
Washington, DC 20202
(202) 732-1265

SERVICE and INFORMATION

Federal Information Center *see Corp. for National Services*

Government Printing Office
North Capitol & "H" Street Northwest
Washington DC 20401
(202) 512-0132
Distributes federal documents and informational pamphlets.

Mail Preference Service
Direct Marketing Association
P. O. Box 9008
Farmingdale, NY 11735-9014
Stops unwanted mail

National Council on Disability
1234 Massachusetts Ave. NW Ste 103
Washington, DC 20005
(202) 347-1234

National LP Gas Association
1600 Eisenhower Lane
Lisle, IL 60532

Nursing Home Information Service Center
1331 F Street, Suite 500
Washington, D.C. 20004-1171
(202) 347-8800

Organ Donors/Transplants
P.O. Box 13770
Richmond, VA 23225
(800)-24 DONOR (for voice information)
(804) 330-8602 (for answers to questions)

Peace Corps
Wahington, D. C. 20526
(800) 424-8580, ext. 93
Send for pamphlet describing program and how to apply.

React, International, Inc.
242 Cleveland
Witchita, KS 67214
Free leaflet *Getting Help by CB Radio*

SERVICE and INFORMATION

Rehabilitation Services Administration

330 C St, SW
Washington, DC 20202
(202) 727-0955

RV Industry Association (RVIA)

1896 Preston White Dr.
P.O. Box 2999
Reston, VA 22090-0999
(703) 620-6003

Social Security Administration

Office of Disablility
Altmeyer Building
6401 Security Bldg.
Baltimore, MD 21235
(800) 772-1213
(301) 965-3424

Stop Junk Mail Association

3020 Bridgeway, #150
Sausalito, CA 94965

U.S. Customs Service Information

1301 Constitution Avenue Northwest
Washington DC 20229
(202) 927-6724
Provides advice on travel to other countries.

Veterans Administration

810 Vermont Avenue NW
Washington, DC 20420
(800) 831-6515
Medical care and research, education and training, death benefits and rehabilitation for veterans.

Washington Service Bureau, Inc.

655 -15th St. NW, Suite 270
Washington DC 20005
(202) 508-0600
Document retrieval company

SUPPORT: AGING
(Also see Legal)

American Association of Homes for the Aging
901 E. St. NW, Suite 500
Washington, DC 20004-2837
(202) 783-2242

American Association of Retired Persons (AARP)
601 E. Street NW
Washington, DC 20049
(202) 434-2277
Lobby for legislation for elderly. Insurance and educational programs.

Children of Aging Parents (CAPS)
2761 Trenton Road
Levittown, PA 19056
(215) 345-5104
Support and guidance for care-givers through workshops.

Flying Senior Citizens of U.S.A.
96 Tamarack Street
Buffalo, NY 14220.
Promotes over age 50 half fare on trips and tours. Publishes bimonthly
newsletter and directory. Also has speakers bureau.

Foster Grandparents Program See *Volunteers*

National Institute On Aging
(800) 222-2225
(301) 496-1752

National Council On Aging
(409 Third St. S.W., Suite 302A
Washington, D.C. 20024
(202) 479-6653
 (202) 479-1200
National information and consultation center. Sponsors conferences
and workshops. Publishes literature on aging.

Widowed Persons Service (WPS)
1909 "K" Street Northwest
Washington, DC 20049
Program of AARP. National outreach group of volunteers of all ages
who have been widowed. "Directory of Services for Widowed."

SUPPORT: DEATH AND DYING

Choice In Dying

200 Varick St.
New York, NY 10014
(212) 366-5540
Provides information, counseling, publications.

Continental Assn of Funeral & Memorial Societies, Inc.

1828 L St. N.W.
Washington DC 20036
(202) 293-4821
Preplanning a less expensive funeral through memorial societies.

Eye Bank For Sight Restoration

210 East 64th Street
New York, NY 10021
(212) 980-6700
Collects and distributes corneal tissue from donors. Research, pub.

Hemlock Society   See *Legal Help*

The Living Bank (Organ Donors)

P.O. Box 6725
Houston, TX 77265
(800) 528-2971—24 hours a day.
Maintains national registry for organ donors.

National Hospice Organization

1901 N. Moore St., Ste 901
Arlington, VA 22209
(703) 243-5900
Telephone referral service and maintains a directory of hospices.

SUPPORT GROUPS
See Aging and Death

Aides Hotline (800) 342-2437

Al-Anon Family Group Headquarters
(800) 344-2666 in United States
(800) 443-4525 in Canada
Sponsors regional groups for relatives and friends of persons with alcoholic problems. Publishes newsletters, reports, books.

Alcoholics Anonymous (AA) World Services
P.O. Box 22511
Bullhead City, AZ 86439-2511
(800) 864-1606
Publishes books, booklets and sponsors local groups.

Alzheimer's Association (Support Groups)
919 N. Michican Ave., Suite 1000
Chicago, IL 60611
(800) 272-3900

CDC National Clearinghouse for Aides/HIV
P.O. Box 6003
Rockville, MD 20849-6003
(800) 458-5231
Information, literature, and referrals

Children of Aging Parents See *Aging*

Choice In Dying
200 Varick St.
New York, NY 10014
(212) 366-5540
Provides information, counseling, publications.

Emphysema
Call Information Center: (800) 238-7800 or
Medical Management: (800) 322-3300

Helping Smokers Quit
% American Cancer Society
777 Third Avenue
New York, NY 10017
Program for people who want to quit smoking but cannot.

SUPPORT GROUPS

See Aging, Death & Dying, Handicapped, Health organizations,

Homosexual Information Center

115 Monroe St.
Bossier City, LA 71111
(318) 742-4709
Referral, information and education services.

Hospice Supplies Store

200 State Road
S. Deerfield, MA 01373
(800) 646-6460
Information and supplies. Catalog,available.

National Hospice Organization

1901 N. Moore St. Ste 901
Arlington, VA 22209
(703) 243-5900

Parents Without Partners, Inc.

7910 Woodmont Avenue
Washington, DC 20014
(800) 637-7974
(800) 969-4797 for California chapters
Single, widowed, or divorced parents bringing up children alone.

Self-help for Hard of Hearing People (SHHH)

7910 Woodmont Ave., Suite 1200
Bethesda, MD 20814
(301) 657-2248
Provides speakers. Publishes *SHHH* a journal about hearing loss.

BUREAU OF LAND MANAGEMENT
(BLM OFFICES)

National office
BLM Public Affairs Office
1800 "C" Street, N.W.
Washington, DC 20240

Alaska
701 C St. (Box 13)
 Anchorage, AK 99513
(907) 277-1561

Arizona
3707 N. Seventh St.
Phoenix, AZ 85014

California
P.O. Box 1449
Sacramento, CA 95825

Colorado
2850 Youngfield St.
Lakewood, CO 80215

Eastern States
350 S. Picket Street
Alexandria, VA 22304

Idaho
550 W. Fort Street
Boise, ID 83702
(208) 342-2711 Ext 2406

Montana
P.O. Box 36800
Billings, MT 59107

Nevada
P.O. Box 12000
Reno, NV 89502
(702) 784-5496

New Mexico
P.O. Box 1449
Santa Fe, NM 87501

Oregon
P.O. Box 2965
Portland, OR 97208

Utah
324 S. State Street
Salt Lake City, UT 84111

Wyoming
P.O. Box 1828
Cheyenne, WY 82003

FOREST SERVICE REGIONAL OFFICES

When writing to a Region, address letter to: Regional Forester; when writing to National Forest, address letter to The Forest Supervisor.

Alaska
Federal Office Bldg.
P.O. Box 1628
Juneau, AK 99802
Covers all of Alaska.

Eastern
310 West Wisconsin Ave.
Milwaukee, WI 53203
Covers Illinois, Indiana,
Ohio, Maine, Michigan,
Minnesota, Missouri, New
Hampshire, Pennsylvania,
Vermont, W. Virginia, and
Wisconsin.

Intermountain
Federal Building
324 - 25th St.
Ogden, Utah 84401
Covers Idaho, Nevada,
Utah, and Bridger-Teton in
Wyoming.

Northern
Federal Bldg, PO Box 7669
Missoula, MT 59807
(406) 329-3194
Covers panhandle of Idaho
and state of Montana.

Pacific Northwest
319 S.W. Pine Street
P.O. Box 3623
Portland, OR 97208
Covers Oregon and
Washington.

Pacific Southwest
630 Sansome Street
San Francisco, CA 94111
Covers California.

Rocky Mountain
11177 West 8th Avenue
P.O. Box 25127
Lakewood, CO 80225
Covers Colorado, Nebraska,
South Dakota and Wyoming
(except Bridger-Teton.)

Southern
1720 Peachtree Road N.W.
Atlanta, GA 30367
Covers Alabama, Arkansas,
Florida, Georgia, Kentucky,
Louisiana, Mississippi, North
Carolina, South Carolina,
Tennessee, Texas, and Virginia.

Southwestern
Federal Building
517 Gold Avenue, S.W.
Albuquerque, NM 87102
Covers Arizona and New
Mexico.

For a list of addresses for all National Forests, write:
USDA/ Forest Service
Office of Information
P.O. Box 2417
WA, DC 20013

USDA Forest Serv.
517 Gold Ave SW
Albuquerque, NM 87102
(505) 842-3292

OFFICES of STATE PARKS

Alaska

Division of Parks
323 East 4th Avenue
Anchorage, AK 99501
(907) 762-2261

Arizona

State Parks Board
1300 W. Washington St.
Phoenix, AZ 85007
(602) 542-4174

California

Dept of Parks & Rec.
P. O. Box 942896
Sacramento, CA 94296
(916) 445-6477
(800) 444-7275

Idaho

Department of Parks
Capitol Building
Boise, ID 83720
(208) 384-2154

Nevada

State Parks System
201 S Fall St, Room 221
Carson City, NV 89701
(800) 237-0774
(702) 687-4322

Oregon

State Parks Branch
1115 Commercial St.
Salem, OR 97301
(800) 452-5687

Utah

Div of Parks & Rec.
500 S. 455 East
Salt Lake City, UT 84102
(801) 328-6000

Washington

Parks & Recreation
P.O. Box 42650
Olympia, WA 98504
(206) 753-5755
(800) 233-0321

REGIONAL OFFICES
NATIONAL PARK SERVICE

The National Park Service was undergoing considerable address and telephone changes, most of which were undertermined at the time of this printing. To obtain a current list, write or call:

Pacific Western Information Center
National Park Service
Ft. Mason Blvd. #201
San Francisco, CA 94123
(415) 556-0560
(415) 556-4122

STATE TRAVEL INFORMATION

Alabama Tourist Bureau
401 Adams Ave., Suite 126
Montgomery,AL 36104
(800) 252-2262
(205) 334-4169

Alaska Div. Tourism
P.O. Box E-101
Juneau, AK 99811
(907) 465-2010

Arizona Office Tourism
2702 North 3rd St., Ste. 4015
Phoenix, AZ 85004
(800) 842-8257
(602) 230-7733

Arkansas Parks /Tourism
One Capitol Mall
Little Rock, AR 72201
(800) 643-8383 (vacation planner)
(800) 828-8974 (office)
(501) 682-7777

California Office Tourism
P.O. Box 1499
Sacramento, CA 95814
(916) 322-2881

Colorado Tourism Board
P.O. Box 38700
Denver, CO 80238
(800) 433-2656
(303) 592-5410

Connecticut Tourism
865 Brook St.
Rocky Hill, CT 06067
((860) 258-4355
(800) 282-6863

Delaware Tourism Office
P.O. Box 1401 99 Kings Hwy.
Dover, DE 19903
(800) 441-8846
(800) 282-8667 (in Delaware)

Florida Div. of Tourism
126 Van Buren Street
Tallahassee, FL 32301
(800) 925-4234
(904) 487-1462

Georgia Dept of Industry
P.O. Box 1776
Atlanta, GA 30301
(800) 847-4842
(404) 656-3590

Hawaii Visitors Bureau
Waikiki Bus. Plaza Ste.801
Honolulu, HI 96815
(800) 464-2924
(808) 923-1811

Idaho Travel Council
700 W. State St.
P.O. Box 83720
Boise, ID 83720
(800) 635-7820
(208) 334-5515

Illinois Tourist Info
100 W. Randolph St. Ste 3-400
Chicago, IL 60601
(800) 223-0121

Indiana Tourism Div.
One N. Capitol Ave
Indianapolis, IN 46204
(800) 289-6646
(317) 232-8860

STATE TRAVEL INFORMATION

Iowa Depart. Tourism

200 East Grand Avenue
Des Moines, IA 50309
(800) 345-4692
(515) 242-4705

Kansas Tourism Division

700 SW Harrison St., Ste. 1300
Topeka, KS 66603-3957
(800) 2-KANSAS
(913) 296-2009

Kentucky Dept. Travel

500 Mero Street
Frankfort, KY 40601
800) 225-8747
(502) 564-4930

Louisiana Tourism Office

P.O. Box 94291
Baton Rouge, LA 70804
(800) 227-4386
(504) 342-8100

Maine Tourism Division

325 B Water Street
Hallowell, ME 04347
(800) 533-9595 (East coast)
(207) 623-0363

Maryland Office Tourism

45 Calvert Street
Annapolis, MD 21401
(800) 543-1036
(800) 445-4558
(410) 767-3400

Massachusetts Div.Tourism

100 Cambridge Street
Boston, MA 02202
(800) 624-6277
(617) 727-3201

Michigan Travel Bureau

P.O. Box 30226
Lansing, MI 48909
(800) 543-2937
(517) 373-1195

Minnesota Office Tourism

375 Jackson Street
ST. Paul, MN 55101
(800) 657-3700
(612) 296-5029

Mississippi Div. Tourism

P.O. Box 1705
Ocean Springs, MS 39564
(800) 927-6378
(601) 359-3414

Missouri Div. Tourism

Truman Building
308 E. High Street
Jefferson City, MO 65102
(800) 877-1234
(314) 751-4133

Montana Travel Bureau

1424 9th Avenue
Helena, MT 59620
(800) 548-3390
(406) 444-2654

Nebraska Travel/Tourism

P.O. Box 94666
Lincoln, NE 68509
(800) 228-4307
(402) 471-3791

Nevada Tourism Com.

5151 South Carson
Carson City, NV 89710
(800) 237-0774

STATE TRAVEL INFORMATION

New Hampshire Travel
P.O. Box 1856
Concord, NH 03302
(800) 258-3608 (N.E. area)
(603) 271-2666
Skiing—(800) 887-5464

New Jersey Tourism
20 West State St. CN 826
Trenton, NJ 08625
(800) JERSEY-7
(609) 292-2470

New Mexico Tourism
491 Old Santa Fe Trail
Lamy Bldg.
Santa Fe, NM 87503
(800) 545-2070
(505) 827-7400

New York Travel Info.
One Commerce Plaza
Albany, NY 12245
(800) 225-5697
(518) 474-4116

North Carolina Tourism
430 North Salisbury St
 Raleigh, NC 27611
(800) 847-4862
(919) 733-4171

North Dakota Tourism
Liberty Memorial Bldg
604 E. Blvd.
Bismark, ND 58505
(800) 437-2077
(701) 328-2525

Ohio Office Tourism
P.O. Box 1001
Columbus, OH 43216
(800) 282-5393
(614) 466-8844

Oklahoma Tourism Dept
2401 N. Lincoln Blvd.
Will Rogers Bldg. Suite 500
Oklahoma City, OK 73105
(800) 652-6552
(405) 521-2413

Oregon Tourism Div.
775 Summer St. N.E.
Salem, OR 97310
(800) 547-7842
(503) 986-0000

Penn. State Travel Bureau
416 Forum Building
Harrisburg, PA 17120
(800) 847-4872
(717) 787-5453

Rhode Island Dept Tourism
Providence, RI 02903
(401) 277-2601

South Carolina Tourism
1205 Pendleton St.
Columbia, SC 29201
(803) 734-0159

South Dakota Div Tourism
711 East Wells Ave.
Pierre, SD 57501
(800) 732-5682
(605) 773-3301

Tennessee Dept Tourism
P.O. Box 23170
Nashville, TN 37202
(615) 741-2158

Texas Tourist Agency
P.O. Box 12728
Austin, TX 78711
(800) 888-8-TEX
(512) 462-9191

STATE TRAVEL INFORMATION

Utah Travel Council
Council Hall/Capitol Hill
Salt Lake City, UT 84114
(800) 200-1160   (801) 538-1030

Vermont Travel Division
134 State Street
Montpelier, VT 05602
(802) 828-3236

Virginia Division Tourism
101 North 9th Street
Richmond, VA 23219
(800) 847-4882
(804) 786-4484

Washington Tourism Div.
101 General Admin. Bldg,
Olympia, WA 98504-0613
(800) 544-1800 (360) 586-2102

West Virginia Tourism
2101 Washington St East
Charleston, WV 25305
(800) 225-5982
(304) 558-2286

Wisconsin Div. Tourism
P.O. Box 7606
Madison, WI 53707
(800) 372-2737
(608) 266-2162

Wyoming Travel Com.
I-25 at College Dr..
Cheyenne, WY 82002
(800) 225-5996
(307) 777-7777

U.S. ARMY CORPS of ENGINEERS (COE) OFFICES

U.S. Army COE, Public Affairs
20 Massachusetts Ave N.W. Washington, DC 20314

Alaska District	(907) 753-2504
Lower Mississippi Valley Division	(601) 634-5000
St. Louis District	(314) 263-5656
Missouri River Division	(402) 221-3020
New England District	(617) 647-8111
North Atlantic Division	(212) 264-7891
North Central Division	(312) 353-6385
North Pacific Division	(503) 294-7190
Ohio River Division	(513) 684-3002
Pacific Ocean Division	(808) 438-1331
Portland District	(503) 294-7190
Seattle District	(206) 764-3742
South Atlantic Division	(404) 331-6711
South Pacific Division	(415) 332-9690
Southwest Division	(214) 767-8194

Above information from Public Affairs Office
P.O. Box 2711, Los Angeles, CA 90053-2325
(213) 894-5320

TRAVEL in CANADIAN PROVINCES

Alberta Tourism Depart.
10155 -102nd St.
Edmonton, Alberta
T6J 4L6 Canada
(800) 661-8888
(403) 427-4321

**British Columbia
Ministry of Tourism**
Parliament Buildings
Victoria, BC
V8V 1X4 Canada
(800) 663-6000

Manitoba Dept Tourism
155 Carlton St, 7th Floor
Winnipeg, Manitoba R3C 3H8
(800) 665-0040

New Brunswick Tourism
P.O. Box 12345,
Fredericton, New Brunswick
E3B 5C3
(800) 561-0123
(506) 453-3984

New Foundland Tourism
P.O. Box 8730
St. Johns, N.F. A1B 4KZ
(800) 563-6353
(709) 729-2830

NW Territories Tourism
Box 506
 Yellowknife, NWT
 X1A 2N4 Canada
(800) 661-0788
(403) 837-7200

Nova Scotia
2695 Dutch Village Rd. #501
Checkin, Nova Scotia
B3L 4V2 Canada
(800) 565-0000
(902) 425-5781

Ontario Travel
Queens Park
Toronto, Ontario
M7A 2E5 Canada
(800) 668-2746
(416) 314-0944

Prince Edward Island
P.O. Box 940
Charlottetown,
Prince Edward Island
C1A 7M5 Canada
(800) 463-4734
(902) 629-2380

Tourisme Quebec
P.O. Box 20000
Quebec, G1K 7X2
(800) 443-7000

Saskatchewan Tourism
500 -1900 Albert St.
Regina, Saskatchewan
S4P 4L9 Canada
(800) 667-7191
(306) 787-2300

Tourism Yukon
P.O. Box 2703
Whitehorse, Yukon
Y1A 2C6 Canada
(403) 667-5340

AUSTRALIA

Camping in Queensland National Parks & Forests

Qld. National Parks
P.O. Box 155
North Quay, Queensland 4002

TRAVEL in EUROPE

Austria
Information Office
500 -5th Avenue
New York, NY 10110

Belgium
National Tourist Office
745 -5th Avenue
New York, NY 10105

Denmark
Danish Tourist Board
655 Third Ave.
New York, NY 10017

Finland
Finish Tourist Board
655 Third Ave.
New York, NY 10017

France
Gov. Tourist Office
610 5th Avenue
New York, NY 10020

Germany
German Information Center
950 Third Avenue
New York, NY 10022
or
Consulate General
460 Park Avenue
New York, NY 10022

Great Britian
British Tourist Authority
40 West 57th Street
New York, NY 10019

Italy
ENIT
630 -5th Avenue
New York, NY 10111

(The) Netherlands
Board of Tourism
355 Lexington Avenue
New York, NY 10017

Portugal
National Tourist Office
548 Fifth Avenue
New York, NY 10036

Romania
National Tourist Office
573 -3rd Avenue
New York, NY 10016

Spain
National Tourist Office
665 -5th Avenue
New York, NY 10022

Sweden
Swedish Tourist Board
655 Third Avenue
New York, NY 10017

Switzerland
National Tourist Office
608 Fifth Avenue
New York, NY 10020

Turkey
Turkish Tourist Office
500 Fifth Avenue
New York, NY 10036

European Caravan Fed.
Secretary General
P.O. Box 1
Langport, Somerset
Great Britain TA10 9HP
(0458) 251821

EMERGENCY ROAD SERVICE

Many vehicle insurance companies cover only the tow vehicle, not the trailer, so it is wise to subscribe to an emergency road service that handles travel trailers and motor homes. Coverage usually includes delivery of gas, jump-starting a stalled engine, and changing a tire at the site of the breakdown, as well as towing the RV and any attached vehicle to the nearest authorized garage regardless of the distance. You pay for the gasoline or garage, parts and labor. Send for information from the following companies and compare the benefits to see which one best meets your needs.

Foremost (TravelSure) RV Insurance

P.O. Box 3357 Dept. 337
Grand Rapids, MI 49501
(800) 262-0170
Escapees members receive discount.

Good Sam Emergency Road Service

P.O. Box 66937
St. Louis, MO 63166-9908
(800) 847-2886, Extension 5703
Restricted to members of Good Sam Club.

Rapid Response Roadservice Motor Club, Inc.

275 E. Hillcrest Dr., Ste. 204
Thousand Oaks, CA 91360
(800) 404-6868
Provides insurance for 500 RV related organizations like Escapees, but membership in one of them is *not* required.

Road America RV Assist

225 Alcazar Ave.
Coral Gables, FL 33134-9672
(800) 443-4187
Provides insurance for FMCA members.

SAFE Driver Motor Club

P.O. Box 25099
Glendale, CA 91201.
(800) 272-6669.

INSURANCE for FULL-TIME RVERS

Alexander & Alexander

700 Fisher Bldg.
Detroit, MI 48202
(800) 521-2942
 For motor homes and buses. No club membership required.

AllState Insurance

Roger Thomas Agency
Brookhollow Square
Livingston, TX 77351
(409) 327-5626
(800) 736-5622
Full-timer's insurance for vehicles registered in Texas

Caravanner Insurance

8655 East Via De Ventura
Scottsdale, Arizona 85258
(800) 423-4403
No club affiliation necessary. Covers travel trailers only.

Foremost Insurance

P.O. Box 3357
Grand Rapids, MI 49501-3357
(800)262-0170
Covers motor homes and travel trailers with special policy at lower
rate for stationary trailers with a special trip insurance when traveling.

National General Insurance

% Good Sam Club's VIP
P.O. Box 66937
St Louis, MO 63166-6937
(800) 847-2886 Ext. 5703
Only for Good Sam Club members or members of Camp Coast To
Coast who have good driving record. Must move RV at least twice
a year. Also has liability insurance for full-time RVers.

Progressive Insurance

Miller Insurance Agency
'2823 SW Glenhaven
Lake Oswego, OR 97034
In Oregon: (503) 636-6347
out-of state: (800) 622-6347

INSURANCE OUTSIDE U.S.A.

AAA National Headquarters
Foreign Insurance Department
1000 AAA Drive
Heathrow, FL 32746-5063
(407) 444-8586

International Gateway Insurance Brokers
3450 Bonita Rd. Suite 101
Chula Vista, CA 92010-3209
(800) 423-2646 (CA only)
(619) 422-3028

Lewis & Lewis Insurance
8929 Wilshire Blvd., Ste 220
Beverly Hills, CA 90211
(800) 966-6830
(213) 655-6830

Mexico Auto Insurance Services
223 Via de San Ysidro
San Ysidro, CA 92073
800-638-0999
800-345-4701

Point South Mexican Insurance
11313 Edmonson Avenue
Morena Valley, CA 92555
(800) 421-1394 Fax: 9090924-3838

Sanborn's Insurance (Mexican)
(512) 682-3601
Offices located at all American border towns.

RV Tourmasters World Wide Insurance
4401 Harlan Avenue
Waco, TX 76710
(817) 754-2027
(800) 729-1406

Vagabundos del Mar Oxbow Marina
P. 0. Box 824
Isleton, CA 95641
Phone: (707) 374-5511

HEALTH INSURANCE /U.S.A. and OVERSEAS

AARP Medicare Supplement Plan

AARP Correspondence Unit
P.O. Box 13999
Philadelphia, PA 19187-0400.
For members of American Association of Retired Persons.

American Academy of Family Physicians (AAFP)

1740 West 92nd Street
Kansas City, MO 64114.
Free list of doctors and specialists in U.S. and Canada for travelers.

Blue Cross/Blue Shield

676 North Saint Clair Street
Chicago, IL 60611-2927
(312) 440-6000
Hospital and Physician health insurance.

Health Care Abroad

Wallach and Company
243 Church Street N.W., Suite 100-D
Ulenna, VA 22180
(800) 237-6615

Health Care Abroad

923 Investment Bldg
1511 "K" Street Northwest
Washington, DC 20005
(800) 237-6615
Medicare and most health plans do not cover sickness or injuries
outside the U.S. This plan provides insurance for duration of trip.

Internl Assoc for Medical Assistance to Travelers (IAMAT)

736 Center Street
Lewiston, NY 14092
        or
123 Edward Street, Suite 725
Toronto, ONT, M5G 1E2 (Canada)
Send (any amount) donation with your request for this *Overseas
Medical Directory.*

HEALTH INSURANCE/U.S.A. and OVERSEAS

International SOS Assistance, Inc.

P.O. Box 11568
Philadelphia, PA 19116
(800) 523-8930
(215) 244-1500

International Traveler's Assistance Association

P.O. Box 10623
Towson, MD 21204
(800) 732-5309
(301) 296-5225

Medic Alert Foundation

P.O. Box 1009
Turlock, CA 95381-1009
(800) 344-3226
Lifetime membership gives you a wallet-size condensation of your medical history and a bracelet or necklace marked "Alert."

MedReport Corporation

P.O. Box 271780
West Hartford, CT 06107-1780
(800) 236-4915, Dept. 107
(860) 231-2408
Gives physicians and hospitals instant access to your complete medical history any time, anywhere. Includes EKGs, X-ray reports, living wills, and organ donor information

SkyMed International, Inc.

4435 North Saddlebag Trail
Scottsdale, AZ 85251
(800) 475-3633
Emergency medical air transportation service. Discunt to Escapees members.

Supplemental Health Policies

Alex Flores, Customer Service
(805) 566-9191
No major medical, no groups.

LEGAL HELP

American Coalition of Citizens With Disabilities

1012 14th Street NW
 Suite 901
Washington, DC 20005
(202) 628-3470
Represents people with physical, mental, or emotional impairments.
Helps disabled obtain their rights.

Choice In Dying Inc.

200 Varick St.
New York, NY 10014
(212) 366-5540

Concern For Dying

250 West 57th Street
New York, NY 10107
(212) 246-6962
(800) 248-2122
Publishes quarterly newsletter and books re: prevention of pro-longing
dying process. Merged with Society for the Right to Die.

Consumer Protection Center

720 - 20th Street Northwest
Washington, DC 20052
(202) 676-7585
Purpose: To help the consumer. Publishes *Consumer Protection
Reporting Service* twice a year as well as books and a newsletter.

Copyright Clearance Center, Inc.

27 Congress Street
Salem Mass., 01970
(508) 744-3350

Copyright Office

Library of Congress
Washington DC 20559
Purpose: Register claims to copyright. Offers copyright searches and
information on copyright subjects.

LEGAL

Council of Better Business Bureaus
1515 Wilson Blvd.
Arlington, VA 22209
(703) 276-0100
Helps locate correct bureau to turn in a complaint. Must be done at
closest bureau to company's address—not complainer's address.

Digest of Motor Laws
American Automobile Association

Gives rules of licensing and towing. Updated annually $6 ppd.

Direct Marketing Association (DMA)
Six East 43rd Street
New York, NY 10017
(212) 689-4977
Makes companies fulfill obligations on mail orders. Maintains lists of
consumers who don't want junk mail or telephone sales calls.

Federal Trade Commission, Public Reference Branch
6th Street and Pennsylvania Ave NW
Washington, DC 20580
(202) 326-2180
Protects public against deceptive business practices. Does not act on
complaints, but uses them to build cases against companies.

Guns *see NRA under safety*

Hemlock Society
P.O. Box 66218
Los Angeles, CA 90066
(213) 391-1871
Supports active voluntary euthanasia for terminally ill.

Legal Services For the Elderly
132 West 43rd Street, 3rd floor
New York, NY 10036
(212) 595-1340
Research, legislation, and education. Publishes reports quarterly.

LEGAL

The Living Bank *(organ donors)*
P.O. Box 6725
Houston, TX 77265
(800) 528-2971

National Automobile Theft Bureau
390 North Broadway
Jericho, NY 11753
(516) 935-7272
Investigation into and location of stolen vehicles.

Parents Rights On Education
12571 Northwinds Drive
Saint Louis, MO 63141
(314) 434-4171
Supports parents' rights to direct education of their children. Fights against compulsory attendance of public schools.

Pension Rights Center
1346 Connecticut Avenue N.W. Room 1019
Washington, DC 20036
(202) 296-3778
Protects pension rights of workers, retirees, and their families and provides assistance for individuals with pension problems.

Right To Know
P.O. Box 1409
Grand Prairie, TX 75050
Helps adopted people find real parents.

Rules Of The Road *(Published by RVIA)*
14650 Lee Road
Chantilly, VA 22021
State-by-state reference of state laws that apply to RV ownership and highway use. Includes the operating and use requirements and required safety equipment. Write for fee.

Veterans Administration: *See organizations*

MAIL and MESSAGE SERVICES

American Home Base
P.O. Box 2430
Pensacola, FL 32513
(800) 422-4663

Aunt Bee's Mail Service
1400 Colorado Street #C-1
Boulder City, NV 89005
(702) 293- 5361
(800) 484-1041

Blue Skies
P.O. Box 965
Palmetto, FL 34220-0965
(800) 729-4591

Calgary Mail Box Inc.
918 - 16th Avenue N.W.
Calgary, Alberta T2M OK3
(403) 289-1474

**Escapees Mail and
Voice Message Service**
101 Rainbow Drive
Livingston, TX 77351
(800) 231-9896
(409) 327-2870
(for Escapees members)

Fast Forward
Box 917729
Longwood, FL 32791-7729
(800) 321-9950 USA & Canada

FMCA Mail Service
P.O. Box 44209
Cincinnati, OH 45244
(800) 445-1732
(for FMCA members)

Good Sam Club
P.O. Box 11097
Des Moines, IA 50381-1097
(800) 234-3450 (U.S.A.)
(for GS members)

Mail, Messages & More
6301 S. Squaw Valley Rd.
P.O. Box 2190
Pahrump, NV 89041-2190
(800) 722-7468

MCCA, Inc.
1614 SW Seagull Way
Palm City, FL 34990
(800) 525-5304
(407) 288-1360

**NATO (Nat'l Assoc. of
Trailer Owners)**
P.O. Box 1418
Sarasota, FL 34230
(800) 237-NATO

Nomad Services
Box 2530
Homer, Alaska 99603
(907) 235-5538

Oregon Mailing Address
1574 Coburg Rd.
Eugene, OR 97401
(800) 283-0424

Outpost Mail & Message
P.O. Box 185
Wilson, WY 83014
(800) 331-4460

Postal Express
P.O. Box 12769
Salem, OR 97309
(800) 225-6164
(503) 363-2677

**Remail Fast Forward
Message Service**
P. O. Box 917729
Longwood FL 32791
(800) 321-9950
(407) 774-3222

MAIL and MESSAGE SERVICES

St. Brendan's Isle, Inc
60 Canterbury Court
Orange Park, FL 32065
(800) 544-2132

Travelers Overnight Mail Association (TOMA)
Box 2010
Sparks, NV 89431
(702) 331-1500

Travelers Remail Association (TRA)
6110 Pleasant Ridge Rd, Ste. 1
Arlington, TX 76016
(800) 666-6710
(817) 478-9466

Travelers Mail Express
Box 10121
Eugene, OR 97440
(800) 843-7282
(541) 345-5069

Wanderers Mail Service
1916 Pike Place #12
Seattle, WA 98101-1013
(800) 441-5675
(206) 441-5678

MAIL ORDER PHARMACIES

Action Mail-Order Drugs
P.O. Box 787
Waterville, ME 04903
(800) 452-1976

AARP Pharmacy Service
510 King Street, Dept NBA
Box 19229
(800) 456-2226
Dept. 833130
Alexandria, VA 22313

Medi-Mail
P.O. Box 98520
Las Vegas, NV 89193-8520
(800) 331-1458

Price Club/Costco
P.O. Box 270158
San Diego, CA 92198
(800) 726-2456
(for Price Club members)

Mail order drug companies are allowed to refill drugs (except narcotics) and mail to you in all 50 states regardless of location of the doctor who wrote the prescription. They also sell over-the-counter drugs, vitamins, and health care products at a discount.

Filling prescriptions at pharmacies that are located across the country, such as WalMart, generally means you can get the pharmacist at the same chain store in another state to verify by computer and refill for you without getting a prescription from a new doctor.

MEDICAL EQUIPMENT

Hospice Supplies Store
200 State Road
S. Deerfield, MA 01373
(800) 646-6460
Catalog,available.

Medical Equip. Co.
106 Quigley Blvd.
New Castle, DE 19720
(800) 322-3300

Regional Respiratory Co.
Pratt, KS 67124
(316) 672-6429
Oxygen unit in your RV.

PARKING (FREE)

Corp. Of Engineer (COE) Campgrounds
U.S. Army COE, Public Affairs
20 Massachusetts Ave. NW
Washington, DC 20314

Ohio Power Company
P.O. Box 328
McConnelsville, OH 43756
Camp free on 35,000 acres of forested land off I-77 in Morgan
County, Ohio. Write for map and camping permit.

The Slabs (California)
Four miles east of Niland, California, off State Hwy 111, near Salton
Sea in southeastern California. Ask directions in Niland. Free desert
parking (no services) for unlimited periods at old military base.

U.S. Government Printing Office
Superintendent of Documents
Washington DC 20402
Send $1 for listings where camping (usually free) is permitted.

PETS

Pet Information Bureau
666 5th Avenue, Suite 1200
New York, NY 10019
(212) 399-4422
Central clearinghouse for information on pets and their care.

Pet Switchboard
3075 AIhambra Drive, Ste 101
Shingle Springs, CA 95682
(800) 824-7888
 Members get ID tag with
toll-free telephone number.

RV RENTALS

Apex Leisure Limited

273/275 London Road, Staines, Middlesex TW18 4JJ
(0784) 463-233 (overseas) Fax: 0784-463239

Cruise America

7740 Northwest 34th Street, Miami, FL 33122.
(800) 325-0633 or (305) 591-7511
Nationwide motor home rentals. One-way option.

Go Vacations, Limited

Rural Route #3, Highway 50, Bolton, Ontario , Canada, LOP lAO
(416) 857-6281 Serves Canada and U.S. with a one-way option.

Overseas Motorhome Tours

222-K South Irena St., Redondo Beach, CA 90277
(800) 322-2127 or (310) 543-2590

Recreational Vehicle Rental Assn (RVRA)

(Branch of RVIA)
P.O. Box 2999, Reston, VA 22090
(800) 336-0154
Directory lists RV dealers in U.S and Canada for all types RVs.

Travel Home Vacations

20383 #10 Hwy., Langley, B.C. Canada V3A 5E8
(800) 663-7848 or (604) 533-1566

U.K. Motorhomes

High Street, Harlington, Hayes, Middlesex UB3 5DN, England
(018) 759-7943 Fax 081-759-7961

Visit Australia Tours

Eliza Travel Pty. Ltd. P.O. Box 385, Mount Eliza,Vic 3930 (Australia)
Freecall for bookings only: 1-800 338817 International code (613)
Fax: (03) 9787 7194
Motor home rentals in Australia, New Zealand, and Europe.

Worldwide Reservation Center

Global Motorhome Travel Inc.
1142 Manhattan Ave. #300, Manhattan Beach, CA 90266
(800) 468-3876 or (310) 318-9995
Fax (310) 318-9795

SAFETY: AUTO / CONSUMER / FIRE

Also, see safety equipment and legal section

Center For Auto Safety

2001 South Street Northwest, Washington, DC 20009-1160
(202) 328-7700 (Report infractions to them.)

Consumer Protection Center

720 - 20th Street Northwest, Washington, DC 20052
(202) 676-7585
Publishes *Consumer Protection Reporting Service* twice a year.

Consumer Research *(see magazines)*

Fire Safety Associates

P.O. Box 1166, Solana Beach, CA 92075
Heat detector early fire warning. Doubles as security system.

National Fire Prevention & Control Administration

Department of Commerce, Washington DC 20230
Publishes information on fire prevention and a monthly newsletter.

National Highway Traffic Safety Administration

Department of Transportation, Washington, DC 20590
(800) 424-9393
Maintains list of vehicle parts recalls. For purchasers of used vehicles.

National Rifle Association (NRA)

11250 Waples Mill Rd.,Fairfax, VA 22030
Information on state gun laws. Fights for right to own weapons.

National Safety Council

1121 Spring Lake Dr., Itasca, IL 60143-3201
(708) 285-1121
Reports vehicles with unsafe features.

National Transportation Safety Board

490 L'Enfant Plaza East, Washington, DC 20594
(202) 382-6600
Investigates accidents and recommends safety measures.

National Weather Service

Department of Commerce, 8060 13th Street
Silver Spring, MD 20910
Forecasts weather and issues storm warnings.

SCHOOLS and EDUCATION for CHILDREN & ADULTS

American School *(Grades 9 through 12)*

850 East 58th Street
Chicago, IL 60637
(312) 947-3300
Nonprofit. Accredited home-study high school. Offers general and college prep courses with approx. 100 subjects. Write for prices.

Arrowmont School of Arts & Craft *(adults)*

P.O. Box 567
Gatlinburg, TN 37738
(615) 436-5860
Workshops and classes from June to mid-August. Write for details.

Augusta Heritage Arts Workshops

%Augusta Heritage Center
100 Campus Drive
Elkins, WV 26241
(304) 637-1209
Classes run mid-July to mid-August at Daves and Elkins College.

Calvert School *(Kindergarten through 8th grade)*

105 Tuscany Road
Baltimore, MD 21210
(410) 243-6030
For parents who travel or who prefer to teach their children at home.

John Campbell Folk School *(adults)*

Route 1, Box 14A
Brasstown, N.C. 28902
(800) 365-5724
(704) 837-2775
Classes June through August. Campground on campus.

Elderhostel *(Classes for senior citizens over age 60)*

80 Boylston Street, Ste 400
Boston, MA 02116
(617) 426-8056
Education and hosteling with facilities for RVers. Free catalog.

ElderTreks

597 Markham St.
Toronto, Ontario, Canada M6G 2L7
(800) 741-7956 or (416) 588-5000

SCHOOLS and EDUCATION for CHILDREN & ADULTS

Independent Study *(High school and College)*
University of Nebraska-Lincoln
Corporate Clissord Hardin, Room 269
Lincoln, NE 68583-9800
(402) 472-7211
Offers high school and university courses.

Institute of Lifetime Learning
(202) 662-4895
Lists 22 Colleges

Interhostel Educational Travel
6 Garrison Avenue
Durham, NH 03824
People over 50. Two-week schools in Australia, China, and Europe.

International Spanish Institute of Ensenada *(adults)*
% Innoved, U.S. Educational Marketing
9512 Oakridge Place
Chatsworth, CA 91311
(818) 718-0503
Learn Spanish in a total immersion program that includes living with a Mexican family. Classes are in Ensenada, Baja, Mexico.

Penland School of Crafts
Penland, NC 28765
(704) 765-2359

RV Service Technician Schools
RVIA (Recreational Vehicle Industry Assn.)
P. O. Box 2999
Reston, VA 22090-2999
(800) 336-0154
Training courses on RV repairs by National RV Technical Institute.

TEMP JOBS & SELF-EMPLOYMENT

American Entrepreneurs Association
2311 Pontius Avenue
Los Angeles, CA 90064-9976
(213) 478-0437
(800) 421-7296
Monthly magazine for those interested in starting a profitable business.

American Guide Services
P.O. Box 790
Port Angeles, WA 98362
(206) 452-9747
Campground map producer employs travelers who qualify.

Career Employees Service, Inc.
1975 Hempstead Turnpike
East Meadow, NY 11554.
Jobs in clerical and medical fields.

(The) Caretaker Gazette
2380 NE Ellis Way, Ste C-16
Pullman, WA 99163
(509) 332-0806
Some are exchange of site-sitting while landowner goes on vacation,
and others are a job that includes a salary. Subscription $24/yr.

Employers Overload Company
8040 Cedar Avenue South
Minneapolis, MN 55420
Includes office, industrial, marketing, and technical jobs.

Guide to Overseas Opportunities
Educational Travel Directory
P.O. Box 344
Amherst, MA 01004

Hamilton Stores, Inc.
1709 West College
Bozeman, MT 59715
(800) 385-4979
Jobs include food service, grocery, cooks, warehouse, and many other
positions. All Hamilton Stores are at national parks.

TEMP JOBS & SELF-EMPLOYMENT

Home Sitters on Wheels of America, Inc.
5200 Torrey Pines Court/ % George Gallant, Pres.
Carmichael, California 95608
(916) 483-5146
House, pet, and plant sitting full or part time.

Manpower, Inc.
5301 North Ironwood Road, Milwaukee, WI 53201
Temporary work in all fields including office, industrial, technical,
medical, and maintenance jobs.

Rolling Ventures
P.O. Box 2190-1941,Pahrump, NV 89041-2190

Southeast Publications, Inc.
4360 Peters Road, Fort Lauderdale, FL 33317
(800) 832-3292
Sell advertising for campground maps as you travel nationwide.

Sunshine Artist
1736 North Highway 427,Longwood, FL 32750-3410
(800) 597-2573
Contacts and advice for working artists.

Traveling nurses *see next page*

Volunteer Jobs Pub: "Helping Out In the Outdoors"
Box 2514, Lynnwood, WA 98036
Directory ($2) lists 160 agencies in 42 states that use volunteer help.

Workamper News
Greg & Debbie Robus, Publishers
201Hiram Road, Heber Springs, AR 72543-8747
(800) 446-5627
(501) 362-2637
Publication gives temporary and long-term jobs as park managers,
maintenance, drivers, salespeople, tour guides and many others.
Subscription: $23/yr U.S. (six issues) or $29 Canada/Mexico.

Workers On Wheels (WOW)
101 Rainbow Dr. #2174, Livingston, TX 77351
Publication is infromation sharing by those working on the road.
Employment opportunities and site exchanges are listed.

EMPLOYMENT FOR TRAVELING NURSES

(The) Action Group
88 Upham St.
Malden, MA 02148
(800) 343-2177
(617) 321-5793
(Fax: 617-321-8494)

American Mobile Nurses
San Diego Corporate Center
12730 High Bluff Drive, Ste. 400
San Diego, CA 92130
(800) 282-0300
(619) 792-0711
(Fax: 619-792-5956)

Cross Country Healthcare Personnel
1515 South Federal Hwy., Suite 210
Boca Ratan, FL 33432
(800) 347-2264
(407) 394-0088
(Fax: 407-338-3269)

M.R.A. Staffing Systems, Inc.
7771 W. Oakland Park Blvd. #100
Fort Lauderdale, FL 33351
(800) 327-2759
(305) 748-3300
(Fax: 305-572-8829

Medical Express
1650 38th St. Ste. 101E
Boulder, CO 80301
(800) 544-7255
(303) 449-7470
(Fax: 303-449-5313)

Supplemental Health Care Services, Ltd.
2696 Sheridan Drive
Tonawanda, NY 14150
(800) 456-6677
(716) 832-8986
(Fax: 716-832-3407)

VOLUNTEER PROGRAMS

AARP Volunteer Talent Bank

601 E Street NW
Washington, DC 20077-1214

Foster Grandparents Program

806 Connecticut Avenue
Northwest Room M-1006
Washington, DC 20525
(800) 424-8580
Work with retarded and handicapped children. Small stipend.

Four-One-One *(Also known as 411)*

7304 Beverly Street
Annandale, VA 22003
(703) 354-6270
National clearinghouse on volunteerism. Write for information.

Habitat for Humanity International

121 Habitat St.
Americus, GA 31709-3498
(912) 924-6935

Retired Senior Volunteer Program (RSVP)

1201 New York Ave. 9th Floor
NW Washington, DC 20525
(202) 606-5000
Needs volunteers 60 and over who will perform services on regular
basis at local schools, courts, health care, rehab, and meals on wheels.

Traveling Retired American Volunteers (TRAV)

P.O. Box 5645
Hollywood, FL 33083-5645
Exchange free campsite for work on community projects.

Volunteer: The National Center

1111 North 19th Street, Suite 500
Arlington, VA 22209
(703) 276-0542
Bimonthly newsletter encourages volunteerism.

*Also see RV Clubs for Laborers For Christ, Mobile Missionary
Assis. Program, and Servants On Wheels Ever Ready (SOWERS)*

MUSEUMS

The following museums are unique. Each state also has historical societies and museums that specialize in the history of their area.

Alaska State Museum

10 Whittier, Juneau, AK 99801
(907) 586-1224
Art, history,NW Coast Indian art, Alaskan native art, and Alaskans.

American Museum of Immigration

National Park Service Dept of the Interior, Liberty Island, NY 10004
(212) 732-1236. Tells the story of immigration.

American Museum—Hayden Planetarium: Perlun Library

 81st Street and Central Park West, New York, NY 10024
(212) 873-1300
Planetarium and astronomy research library.

Barbed Wire Hall of Fame

Box 327, Blockton, IA 50836
(515) 788-3641
 Display of barbed wire with its history.

Boys Town PhilaMatic Center

Box 1, Boys Town, NE 68010
(402) 498-1360
Stamp, coin, and currency museum.

Branford Trolley Museum

17 River Street, East Haven, CT 06512
(203) 467-6927
Antique electric railway cars. Has trolley ride for tourists.

Brigham City Museum-Gallery

Box 583, Brigham City UT 84302
(801) 723-6769
History of Mormons and Utah pioneer period.

Buffalo Bill Museum

Box 284, LeClaire, IA 52753

Canal Museum

Weighlock Bldg, Erie Blvd. East, Syracuse NY 13202
(315) 471-0593
Exhibits, tours, and lectures on history of canals in America.

MUSEUMS

Carnegie Museum of Natural History

4400 Forbes Avenue ,Pittsburgh, PA 15213
(412) 622-3328
Dinosaurs, art, health, medicine, history, nature, and science.

(The) Children's Museum

30th and Meridian Streets,Indianapolis, Indiana 46208
(317) 294-5431
Education through participatory programs and exhibits.

Circus World Museum

426 Water Street, Baraboo, WI 53913
(608) 356-8341

Collier State Park Logging Museum

Box 428, Klamath Falls, Oregon 97601
Evolution of logging equipment.

Conneaut Railroad Museum

324 Depot Street, Conneaut, OH 44030
(216) 599-7878
Historic artifacts & equipment of steam railroad era.

Conner Prairie Pioneer Settlement

30 Conner Lane, Noblesville, IN 46060
(317) 773-3633
Indiana life in the 1830s with live demonstrations.

Fort Lewis Military Museum

Bldg 4320, Fort Lewis, WA 98406
(206) 967-4796
Interprets and exhibits the military history of the Northwest.

45th Infantry Division Museum and Library

2145 Northeast 36th Street, Oklahoma City, OK 73111
(405) 424-5313
History of Oklahoma citizen/soldier & Choctaw Indian tribal police.

Great Plains Black Museum

Archives & Interpretive Center, 2213 Lake St., Omaha NE 68110
(402) 344-0350
Black museum of homesteaders & cowboy in the Great Plains area..

MUSEUMS

Greenfield village/Henry Ford Museum

Dearborn, Michigan 48121
(313) 271-1620
Largest indoor-outdoor museum in America.

Hershey Museum of American Life

1 Chocolate Avenue, Hershey Pennsylvania 17033
(717) 534-3439
German settlers and story and tour of Hershey's chocolate

Historic New Orleans Collection

533 Royal Street, New Orleans Louisiana 70130
(504) 523-7146
Pictorial material covers New Orleans from 17th to 20th century.

Institute of American Indian Arts Museum

Cerrillos Road, Santa Fe, NM 87501
(505) 988-6281
Museum and Native American videotape archives for research.

International Museum of Photography

George Lastman House, 900 E. Ave., Rochester NY 14607
Collection spans history of photography from 1839 to date.

International Tennis Hall of Fame & Museum

Newport Casino, Newport, Rhode Island 02840
(401) 849-3990
Exhibits of tennis trophies and memorabilia.

The Jewish Museum

1109 5th Avenue ,New York, NY 10028
(212) 860-1888
Museum of Judaic art, history and Jewish culture.

John Young Museum & Planetarium (JYMP)

810 E, Rollins Street, Orlando, Florida 32803
(305) 896-7151
Hands-on museum covers nature and science.

Kendall Whaling Museum

Box 297, Sharon, Massachusetts 02067
(617) 784-5642.
Exhibits art, artifacts, and books on whales and seals.

MUSEUMS

MacArthur Memorial
MacArthur Square, Norfolk, Virginia 23510
(804) 441-2256
The General's letters, reports, messages and library.

Marine Corps Museum
Marine Corps Historical Center, Headquarters (Code H.D.)
Washington DC 20380
(202) 433-3840
John Phillip Sousa's collection. Focus is on amphibious warfare.

(The) Mariners Museum
1 Museum Drive ,Newport News, VA 23606
(804) 595-0368
Man's relationship to the sea. Models, photos and reference library.

Metropolitan Museum of Art
5th Avenue at 82nd Street
New York NY 10028
History of art from ancient times to present.

Museum of African Art
 Eliot Elisofon Archives, 316-318 A Street Northwest
Washington DC 20002
(202) 547-6222
Collection of photographs of African art and culture.

Museum of Anthropology
University of Missouri, 104 Swallow Hall
Columbia, Missouri 65211
(314) 882-3764
Exhibit of artifacts made by man in different cultures.

Museum of Modern Art
11 West 53rd Street, New York, NY 10019
(212) 956-6100
Collection of the best works in modern art.

Museum of Repertoire Americana
Route 1, Mt Pleasant, Iowa 52353
(319) 385-8937
Pictures, posters, memorabilia from opera house and tent theaters.

MUSEUMS

Museum of Confederacy

1201 East Clay Street, Richmond, Virginia 23219
(804) 649-1861
Confederate history and depository of manuscripts.

Museum of Transportation

300 Congress Street, Boston, Massachusetts 02110
(617) 426-7997
Transportation as it relates to our American social history.

Musical Museum

South Main Street, Deansboro, NY 13328
(315) 841-8774
Early musical instruments. Also antique oil lamps.

National Air & Space Museum

6th & Independence Ave. SW, Washington, DC 20560
(202) 381-4222
Preservation and exhibition of the history of flight.

National Baseball Hall of Fame & Museum

Box 590, Cooperstown, NY 13326
(607) 547-9988
Memorabilia, displays, films, and library.

National Colonial Farm

Route 1, Box 697, Accokeek, Maryland 20607
(301) 283-2113
Re-creation of the 18th century middle-class tobacco plantation.

National Cowboy Hall of Fame

17OO Northeast 63rd Street, Oklahoma City, OK 73111
(405) 478-2250
Ranching. Western performers, and rodeo history.

National Gallery of Art

Constitution Avenue & 6th Street NW, Washington, DC 20007
(202) 737-4215
Western Europe from 13th century. Tours, films, concerts, lectures.

Peabody Museum of Natural History

Yale University, 170 Whitney Ave.,New Haven Conn. 06520
(203) 432-4478 or 432-4044
Dinosaur hall and anthropology exhibits. Art, history, nature, travel.

MUSEUMS

The Phillips Collection
Office Public Affairs, 1600-1612 -21st St. NW Washington, DC 20009
(202) 387-2151
Oldest museum of modern art in U. S. Covers art and music.

Pro Football Hall of Fame
2121 Harrison Avenue NW, Canton, Ohio 44708
(216) 456-8207
Professional football greats of the past.

Remington Gun Museum
Remington Arms Co., Ilion, New York 13357
(315) 894-9961
Firearms manufacturer with an in-plant gun museum.

Ringling Brothers Circus Museum
5401 Bayshore Road, Sarasota, Florida 33578
(813) 355-5101
Authentic circus museum.Parade wagons, posters, and memorabilia.

Shaker Museum
Shaker Museum Road, Old Chatham, NY 12136
(518) 794-9100
Finest Shaker-made artifacts in the world.

Smithsonian Institute
Washington D. C. 20560

U.S. Air Force Museum
Wright-Patterson AFB, Dayton, Ohio
(518) 255-3284
Covers history of military aviation.

Will Rogers Museum
Box 157, Claremore, Oklahoma 74017
(918) 341-0719
Preserve memory and promote the spirit of Will Rogers.

Yesteryear Museum
Box 1890 M, Morristown, New Jersey O7960
(201) 386-1920
Music boxes, nickelodeons, player pianos, photographs, etc.

Encyclopedia Index

Index

Index